OUTPERFORM

T H E **N O R M**

for
SALES

The
50 **Best Tips
EVER**
for **Successful Selling**

SCOTT WELLE   *#1 Best Selling Author*

To Dad, the greatest salesman I've ever known.

Want to reach the highest sales level?
Then please check out this *NEW* video...

Yes, it's Complimentary

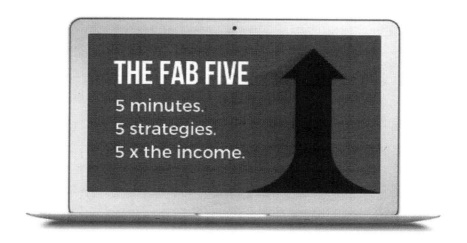

THE FAB FIVE

Five Things ALL Great Salespeople Do Differently...and Better

This book contains my 50 best tips EVER for sales (actually, it contains 60 tips). I realize that can be overwhelming and if you'd like to know where to start, watch this video. No sales pitch here or a hidden agenda to buy a higher-priced program – just 100% actionable content to accelerate your sales results.

5 minutes. 5 strategies. 5 x the income.

For Instant Access go to:

OutperformTheNorm.com/sales

INTRODUCTION

Have you ever wondered what makes a great salesperson? What do they do differently? What makes people buy? What makes people object? How can you get more sales in less time? How do you "close" a prospect and ask for the sale? How do you differentiate your product, service or idea? Why will no one call you back?

This book contains the answers to these questions.

If you're reading this book, you're either already working in sales or contemplating a job that involves selling. Congratulations! You've got some guts. I've never seen a 'true" sales position that is strictly salaried. Most are salary + commission, or straight commission alone.

You're the variable in the sales income equation.

Just so we're clear on terminology, you'll hear "Outperformer" used often throughout this book. Outperformers are located at the intersection of high achievement and fulfillment and are driven to perform their best, personally and professionally. "The Norm" is the opposite breed of animal. They're located at the intersection of comfort and security and are content performing at the status quo.

The Norm can't handle sales. They show up at their 8-5 job, sit at their desk, and collect their guaranteed monthly income. I once heard, "salaried employees will work just hard enough to keep from getting fired and your boss will pay you just enough to keep you from quitting." True statement.

By no means am I advocating that every salaried employee is lazy but sales is different. You get paid what you EARN and what you DESERVE. You have no guaranteed monthly income, and if you do have a base salary, it is probably not enough for you to live your "ideal" lifestyle. You're content writing your own guarantee by your work ethic, skill development and tangible results. Isn't this the way it should be? I live with the crazy notion that we'd have much stronger, harder-working employees if *everyone's* compensation was partially commission-based. It keeps you motivated and accountable.

To join the ranks of the sales Outperformers, you've got to master the fundamental skills. For some, the skills come easier. They are born extraverts and are better communicators. It's like talent in sports—some athletes are genetically predisposed with more hand-eye coordination. They're born on third base. For others, developing the skills requires more effort. But everyone can improve their sales skills if they understand what it *really* takes to succeed. Selling isn't rocket science – it's the consistent, focused practice of the essential skills that drive *real* sales results.

The first basic, most widely misunderstood principle: it doesn't matter how good your product is. Yes, you heard me correctly. It's a cliché that a product sells itself. NOTHING sells itself. If products did sell themselves, what are we here talking about? Certain products, services or ideas do have distinct beneficial advantages but it still takes a highly skilled salesperson to bring them out. Without this, even the best product dies on the vine. Even a product you buy on Amazon still needs a human to upload the images, write the headline and draft the sales copy.

There are three central components to being a sales Outperformer: *Psychology, Productivity* and *Persuasion.* The book is divided into these sections.

In a nutshell, this is what is included:

Psychology is what you think and how you think about it. It's conditioning your mind for sales success. Harnessing the strength of your thoughts.

Productivity is what you do and how you do it. Doing the right things and doing the things right. Being targeted and maximally efficient and effective with your time.

Persuasion is what you communicate and how you communicate it, online and offline. Influencing others through the psychology of our buying behaviors.

Master these three sections and you'll master sales.

This book is a collection of my best strategies to take your sales results to the next level. The tips are cut and dry, with very little fluff. Some of them you're probably executing exceptionally well right now, some you're performing status quo (but could still be improved upon), and others you may not even be aware of.

**The true champion spends more time
working on weakness than showing off strength.**

It's the culmination of these skills that makes a sales Outperformer. This book gives you a step-by-step, easy-to-digest guide of what the best salespeople in the world do to perform at the highest level...and stay there.

Let's GO!

CONTENTS

SECTION 1

PSYCHOLOGY

"Your mind is your greatest asset
or your largest liability."

"This is the last time!"

I met Steve eight weeks ago when I spoke at a large networking breakfast. I remember stepping off the stage, not feeling like I gave my best presentation, but certainly one that I deemed above average.

There was a short line of people at my table in the back of the room wanting to buy books. I noticed a clean-cut, slightly graying gentlemen in a black suit, patiently waiting for his turn to get to the front.

"Hi Scott, my name is Steve. I loved your presentation. I have to get to another meeting but here's my business card. Please get in touch with me—I'd love to have you speak to my team of financial advisors."

Normally I'm prompt with my follow up but this breakfast was on a Friday morning, so I waited until Monday to call him.

Voicemail.

"Hi Steve, this is Scott Welle. It was great speaking with you last Friday morning. I'd love to discuss helping your team of financial advisors Outperform. Please give me a call back at your earliest convenience."

After four days, still no response. Later that week, on *Follow Up Friday*, I send him an email reiterating the same exact message I left on his voicemail.

Once again, no response. I leave him another voicemail the following week, emphasizing that I'd love to work with him and mentioning some of the other training I'd done with financial firms (always a good sales strategy).

This process continues with 4 more contacts via voicemail or email over the next 6 weeks. As you can probably guess, I hear nothing back from Steve.

Not. One. Word.

If you contacted a prospect 7 times during an 8-week period and received *no response*, what would you be thinking?

Not interested? Doesn't like you? Is doing business with a competitor?

All of these are valid thoughts and I'd be lying if I say that some of them aren't creeping into my psychology. But I'm a stubborn German and he TOLD me that he wanted to do business with me! I'm not giving up.

I email Steve one last time.

I receive a response ten minutes later. "Scott, I'm so sorry. My executive assistant went on maternity leave and I'm absolutely buried. But I want to do business with you—can you meet for a coffee tomorrow?"

Steve is alive! The next day we meet for coffee and set the date for a future training for his team. I'm still in a state of shock as we shake hands to close the meeting.

Life is about narratives, or the stories we tell ourselves. Sales Outperformers tell better stories. In this case, most sales studies say that you have to contact a prospect a *minimum* of 6 times to get a meeting (or phone call), yet how many of us are willing to tell ourselves that story when Steve is missing in action and unresponsive?

PSYCHOLOGY creates the thought patterns that you need to Outperform and makes your mind your greatest sales asset.

1. PRACTICE MAKES PERMANENT

Great salespeople practice their craft. It's a misconception that someone is born to be a salesperson. Sure, an extroverted personality and communication style may come easier to some but it is still something that needs to be developed through hard work and practice.

Think about it in regards to athletics – even the most talented athletes are never going to get to the pros without honing their skills through hours and hours of practice. Talent alone is never enough. It may speed up or slow down the learning curve but that's about it. Talent is given. Skills are earned.

Selling is exactly the same way. If you've got a huge meeting, pitch or proposal coming up, how well are you going to perform if you go into the game without ever having practiced?

Role-playing is practice for salespeople.

I'll be the first to say, I HATE role-playing (and almost everyone else does to). We hate it because you inevitably get asked a question or put on the spot where you end up not having an answer and you look like a moron. So, it begs the question, would you rather potentially look like a moron in front of someone who is trying to help you or in front of your prospect? It's an obvious choice.

The single most important aspect of role-playing is to ask all relevant questions and to state all possible objections. Leave no stone unturned. And, if you're role-playing, treat it like you're in the game. Don't give a half-assed effort because you know it "doesn't count." It DOES count. Practice doesn't make perfect – practice makes PERMANENT. Only perfect practice makes perfect.

So, role-play with the same effort, intensity and focus that you would as if it were game day. This is a defining characteristic between sales professionals and sales amateurs.

Outperforming Sales Strategy

The more realistic you can make role-playing, the better prepared you'll be when game day comes. Make the full pitch, talk how you'd normally talk and wear what you'd normally wear. Each of these things will build familiarity, and with familiarity comes confidence. A basic tenet of Outperformers is that practice conditions mirror performance conditions as closely as possible.

If you want an additional leg up, record yourself doing it. If it's a call, fire up your phone and record the audio. How's your tonality? Certainty? If it's an in-person meeting, use video. How's your body language? Persuasion? Would YOU buy from you?

Without role-playing, it becomes awfully difficult to accurately answer these questions.

2. THIS PRECEDES MOTIVATION

What's your purpose for being in sales? If you don't know it, spend a minute or two *really* thinking about it. Don't give a surface answer; REALLY think about why you're in sales and what you'd like to get from it.

Is it money? That's a good start but WHY do you want the money? Get out of debt? Vacations? College fund for your kids? New car or house?

Is it significance? Again, this is a good start but WHY do you crave significance? To leave a legacy? Or have ego and notoriety? Want to change the lives of others?

I often tell clients: "A powerful purpose precedes motivation." It's what gets you up earlier and has you stay later, even — and especially — when you don't feel like it.

By asking yourself these deep, introspective questions, you'll gain emotional leverage (one of the most powerful factors in goal achievement) on why sales matters to you. It is fuel for your motivational fire when you don't feel like making a call, sending an email, giving a presentation or attending an event.

One of the biggest clichés in self-help is "finding your purpose." I've never liked that term. It sounds like if you just wander around for long enough, you'll eventually find your purpose like a missing sock that was accidentally left in the dryer.

A purpose isn't something you find; it's something you CREATE.

The creation of this purpose comes from connecting where you are now to the future you're going to have if you continue down your current path. Is this where you want to be? Is this how you want your life to look?

Years ago a famous research study was done at Stanford on success and delayed gratification. They brought in kids and offered them a marshmallow (they replicated the study with cookies also). They had two options — eat the marshmallow immediately, or if they were willing to wait 15 minutes, the experimenter promised to bring them a second marshmallow.

The researchers followed the kids over time and found that the ones who were able to delay gratification by waiting the 15 minutes were significantly more successful in the long term.

Outperforming Sales Strategy

Sales operates on a similar principle. Positive actions today don't usually pay off with immediate gratifications. There's an inevitable delay and most people don't have the "futuristic" mindset to be able to link what they're doing now to the impact it will have later.

So, what's your purpose? It can't just be for the paycheck or the commissions. These things won't sustain. Whatever your purpose is, create it, hold onto it and remind yourself of it *daily*. A strongly CREATED purpose precedes and drives motivation.

3. YOU'RE THE CEO

When you're in sales, you're working in a business within a business (assuming you don't actually *own* the business). You may not realize it, but everyone's salaries depend on you making sales. What you do *matters* to the greater organization.

You need to adopt the mentality that you're CEO of your own sales business. Everyone is relying on you and it's up to you to determine how to most effectively and efficiently operate your business. This means having a strategic plan for growth and having the right people in the right places. Even if you don't have to DO everything in your sales business (hopefully you've delegated accordingly), you still have to KNOW everything that is happening in your business. That's how CEOs do it.

If you're a solopreneur (the only one responsible for making sales), you still need to have a strategic plan and leverage your time accordingly. You also need to understand that, as your sales grow, so will the need to seek additional support. There's only so much you can do alone.

Outperforming Sales Strategy

If you're the CEO of your sales business, how are you stacking up right now? If, tomorrow, they were going to run a front-page story on you in *USA Today* or *The Wall Street Journal* (like they would for the CEO of any major company), would you be comfortable with them writing the story? What would they say? How would you answer the questions when you're interviewed? Would you stand tall and be proud of your results?

Adopting a "CEO mentality" means you take specific ownership for the results and production in your sales business. The Norm corporate salesperson will say, I work for *The Best Company Ever*, but you don't work for *The Best Company Ever* – you work for YOURSELF. *The Best Company Ever* just happens to be the name that appears on your paychecks.

Take responsibility and ownership for everything that happens in your sales business. Operate like you're the CEO.

4. DRIVE AND THRIVE

You condition your mind the same way you condition your body – through consistent, daily positive activity. The only way to build something to last is to do it repeatedly over time.

What you feed your brain matters. You can positively condition your psychology to expect success and see the glass as half full, or you can negatively condition it with the greed, scandal and corruption that normally consumes our media and news programming. It's your CHOICE. In fact, if you don't have the results in your life right now that you currently want, your psychological conditioning is probably holding you back. What else could it be?

Outperforming Sales Strategy

The average person spends 500-1000 hours in the car each year. Depending on your type of sales position, you might even spend *more* than this amount of time. What are YOU listening to? Music on your phone? Your favorite satellite station? Talk radio?

500-1000 hours is the equivalent of a *university level education* each year. With the ease of getting audiobooks and audio programs (all of mine are available through Amazon, Audible and iTunes, which are the big players), feeding your mind with whatever you want to has never been easier.

If you're not where you want to be personally and professionally, invest this time wisely in *quality audio* that will positively condition your psychology. My favorites are Brian Tracy, Jim Rohn and Tony Robbins. Immerse yourself fully in whatever skill you want to develop (confidence, self-discipline, achievement, communication, etc.) and continue practicing these activities, consistently. You will reap the sales rewards.

5. EXPECT TO WIN

I have a simple philosophy that I tell all my clients:

"Expect the best; Prepare for the worst."

Expecting the best means you should expect to win. You should expect to make every sale. If the goal of selling is to make a sale, why would you expect anything different?

Sales Outperformers **expect** that people will buy. Sales Amateurs **hope** that people will buy. You might think it's a subtle distinction but it means EVERYTHING.

Much of life is based around a self-fulfilling prophecy – you get back what you put out in the world. If you focus on making sales, you'll find yourself making many more sales. Contrast this with those who hope for it or go into meetings and presentations focusing on not "losing the sale." Even if it's something you're trying to avoid, you're still focusing on the wrong thing.

The necessary counterpoint to expecting the best is also to prepare for the worst. The death of many salespeople has been in not being prepared for people to say no, which will happen, regardless of how good you are at selling.

The importance of preparing for the worst is that you reduce your emotional attachment to the result. There's nothing worse than getting told NO when you were 100% sure the person was going to say YES. Think about how it felt if a boyfriend or girlfriend broke up with you and caught you totally off guard. Not preparing for the worst is just like that...and it gets people into trouble.

Outperforming Sales Strategy

Expecting the best requires using a different language...when speaking to yourself and to others. This is an excerpt from my book, **Outperform The Norm**, on some of the defining characteristics. Pay attention to this language and you'll be consciously, and unconsciously, programming yourself for winning.

THE NORM	OUTPERFORM
HOPEFULLY	DEFINITELY
WHEN I HAVE TIME	I'LL MAKE IT A PRIORITY
EXCUSES	ACCOUNTABILITY
FIXED MINDSET	GROWTH MINDSET
COMFORTABLE	CHALLENGED
SECURE DECISIONS	CALCULATED RISKS
SOMEDAY	TODAY
GIVEN	EARNED
EASY WAY	BEST WAY
RESOURCES	RESOURCEFULNESS
PLAYING NOT TO LOSE	PLAYING TO WIN
FOCUSED ON ME	FOCUSED ON WE
FOLLOWER	LEADER

OUTPERFORMTHENORM.COM

6. IF AT FIRST YOU DON'T SUCCEED

You've probably heard the phrase:

"If at first you don't succeed, try, try again!"

Nowhere is it truer than in sales.

Most sales research will say that someone has to be exposed to a product, idea or service 6-8 times before they will say yes. The sad thing is, The Norm salesperson will never get to this point. They'll think after the second, third, or fourth time that the prospect is simply not interested and they'll give up. Or they'll lose their confidence because they didn't hear an immediate YES. Either way, they won't reach the number of exposures necessary to get the job done.

The one non-negotiable characteristic of sales Outperformers is perseverance. They stick and stay and don't give up. Personally, I look at it the same way I used to when I was an athlete. As long as you leave everything out there on the court, course or field, you can walk away KNOWING you gave your best effort and accept any result. But if you give up too early, have you *really* given it your best effort? Couldn't you have hung in there a little longer to see if it would have panned out?

I'm not advocating you waste your time on a prospect that is genuinely not interested, but there is something to be said for not giving up. It surprising how often a prospect may come around if you're willing to keep after it.

Outperforming Sales Strategy

If you're going to approach a new prospect about your product, idea or service, commit to a plan of action, based on the research of 6 exposures being necessary to make a sale. When you do this, you prep your mind for the process. You prep it that you're in it for the long haul and it's going to take more than just one phone call or email.

Map out a tentative timeline of when you'll contact the prospect during this process. Yes, prepare yourself mentally that they may not respond to your first or second email or voicemail (God forbid that!). But hold yourself accountable to follow through on your plan of action until it's completed. You'll see your sales improve and you'll be astounded the number of sales you make on the fourth, fifth or sixth contact.

7. SELLING WITH PASSION

Kids are sales Outperformers. They passionately plead for mom or dad to buy them something, they create a sense of urgency for why they have to have it NOW and they are masters at selling to someone's emotions.

We can all learn from kids. When I was younger, I knew *exactly* how to speak to my mom to get what I wanted (usually a toy or a candy bar). I was confident, I was bold and I was manipulative. My mother didn't stand a chance :)

Outperforming Sales Strategy

I'm not saying we should manipulate prospects but what we can learn from kids is *"passionate selling."* When you're so passionate about wanting something so badly, the opposite person can't help but give it to you. So, when you're passionate about why a prospect HAS TO have your product, idea or service, what you say matters very little. Kids don't worry about sounding scripted. Passion trumps all.

Keep this visual in your mind when you're on calls, in meetings or conducting presentations. How would a kid be selling your product, idea or service? Would they be selling more passionately and emotionally than you are? Would they be more confident and bold? Would they not take no for an answer?

Good things for all of us to remember.

8. THE PRICE OF ADMISSION

In **Outperform The Norm**, I talk about the Price of Admission, which are the discipline, dedication and sacrifices necessary to achieve a goal. The loftier the goal, the higher the Price of Admission. Great accomplishments require great sacrifices.

Selling is not an easy profession. As stated in the introduction, most people can't handle sales. They can't take the rejection, the uncertainty, the fear of not earning a commission vs. a guaranteed higher salary and the fast-paced, high-stress atmosphere. There's a large Price of Admission in sales.

Think of the Price of Admission as currency. When you walk into a store, you can see on the price tag what a product costs.

Nothing is hidden. The price tag of an item is a representation of its value. More valuable things command a higher price.

The Price of Admission for anything you want to accomplish is sometimes less obvious, but no less important. The general currency, in this case, is your discipline, dedication, sacrifices, mindset, energy and resourcefulness.

Outperforming Sales Strategy

Do you KNOW what you want and your Price of Admission to make it happen?

Selling is a numbers game. Your pay structure is in some way tied to the number of sales you make. Knowing what you want is usually an average monthly dollar amount or a total annual income. Once you know this number, you can reverse engineer it to determine how many sales you'd need to make to reach your desired income level.

But this still doesn't tell you your Price of Admission.

The Price of Admission is how many calls you need to make, how many hours you have to work, how many meetings you need to have, how prospects you need to convert to customers and the amount of personal and professional development you must do to improve your sales skills.

So, the question is, do you KNOW this Price of Admission? If you don't (which is often the case), find someone who does. Find someone who has what you want. They don't have to work for your company or even sell the same type of product, idea or service. Find someone who has been successful in sales and ask them what Price of Admission they paid and what you'd need to do to get the job done. It's THAT simple, but surprisingly few people do it. They run into the woods blind and try to figure it out for themselves. But most people are generous and more than willing to share their advice...if you're willing to seek it out. There's no need to reinvent the wheel. Success duplicates.

9. PRESS ON

Responding to adversity is the only way to become a sales Outperformer. What makes responding to adversity difficult is that we're emotional creatures (yes, men, I'm talking to you too!). It doesn't matter how thick your rhinoceros skin is, when someone tells you NO, it's difficult not to take it personally. In fact, the prospect is not saying NO to you – they're saying NO to your product, idea or service. These are two totally different things, but in our emotional eyes, they may as well be the same thing.

Every single successful Outperformer has had to respond to adversity and press on at some point in their career. Walt Disney was fired from the Kansas City Star because he lacked imagination. Steve Jobs was fired from his own company, Apple, before coming back to change the industry. Oprah Winfrey was fired from a news show because she didn't have camera presence. Abraham Lincoln lost seven elections for public office before becoming president.

Your ability to press on has nothing to do with being an unemotional robot. Some people preach this, claiming, *"just don't take it personally."* Yeah, right. As long as we're human beings who are driven by emotion (and not logic), this is fighting against our basic human instincts. Better to accept it and find a constructive way to move past it.

Outperforming Sales Strategy

Ask yourself the following question:

"Why am I in sales in the first place?"

Whatever the answer is to this question, constantly remind yourself of it. It's your purpose. If you lose a sale and you let it affect you, shame on you. That says more about you than it does about them. No one gets in your head unless you allow them to get in it. They may have the gun but you allow them to pull the trigger.

Responding to adversity in sales comes from remembering your purpose for why you're doing it in the first place. Maybe it's to provide for your family, or buy a new car, or take a vacation, or pay off debt, or prove someone wrong, or contribute to humanity. ANY of these are sufficient reasons. Only YOU know what your purpose is, but after you've accepted your basic emotional reaction to adversity, the faster you can remind yourself of your bigger purpose, the faster you can press on and make the next sale.

10. BE ACCOUNTABLE

Accountability is a key characteristic to being a sales Outperformer. We ALL need to be held accountable for the things we do...and the things we don't do. No blaming, no excuses, no rationalizing, no justification. Just acceptance that we're responsible for our actions and results.

In 2009, I had just started my job as a Regional Account Manager. I was in "outside sales," which basically meant I was responsible for hunting and finding new business. I had two other people I was managing, who were "inside sales," which meant they were responsible for order entry, follow up calls and growth of existing business.

Like most jobs, my first couple months were a blur and I was running around like a chicken with its head cut off. But there was one huge proposal for a school district west of Chicago for about $250,000 that the previous account manager had put together. The proposal was about 80% finished and even though it was by far my largest deal on the table, I let one of my inside sales people look it over and tell me when it needed to be submitted. I was busy trying to figure out what the heck I was doing and learn the ins and outs of my new position.

Well, it turns out that my person misread the due date. She thought it was two weeks later than when it was. OUCH. I didn't even get to submit the proposal because we missed the deadline, which meant we weren't even being considered with the other bidding companies. It was only through a frantic flurry of calls and emails that they agreed to cut me some slack and allow me to complete my proposal. Thankfully, we still got the deal.

I can remember initially being so angry and making so many excuses, but at the end of the day, whose fault was it?

Mine.

I was the Regional Account Manager and I should have personally looked over the proposal. I had nobody to blame but myself. I was accountable.

Outperforming Sales Strategy

Assume total accountability for everything that happens in your sales business. It doesn't matter if you're flying solo or if you're managing a large sales team. If something doesn't get done, regardless of whether it was your direct responsibility, it still falls on your shoulders.

This doesn't mean you have to micromanage every single thing you possibly can. Lots of sales managers want to do this because they're afraid of letting go (and they usually work 80 hours a week and burn out in the process). You just have to be *aware* of everything that's happening in your sales business (even the smaller deals) and take responsibility for the results that come of it. Being accountable is more of a mindset and an attitude. If your attitude is one of not rationalizing, justifying, blaming or excuses, you're well on your way to being a sales Outperformer.

11. LOVE YOUR COMPETITORS

I'm a stubborn, aggressive German with strong beliefs (I'm sure this comes as a big shock to you!). I was raised to stand up for what you believe in and if you want something, you should fight for it.

For the most part, this has served me well. One area where it didn't serve me well was in dealing with sales competitors.

It would usually start with a prospect asking one of the following questions:

"Tell me why your product, idea or service is better than The Next Best Company Ever."

Or...

"The Next Best Company Ever has a product, idea or service that is better than yours."

Or my favorite...

"Someone from The Next Best Company Ever said I shouldn't do business with your company."

You can probably guess where this was going.

In my early sales days, the stubborn, aggressive German would come out swinging! And, instead of speaking passionately about the benefits of my product, idea or service, I would waste my time and energy tearing down The Next Best Company Ever and listing all the reasons why the prospect *shouldn't* do business with that company.

How do you think that made me look? I cringe just thinking about it.

Outperforming Sales Strategy

Always take the high road, plain and simple.

If someone is baiting you on with questions about why your product, idea or service is better than someone else's, handle it with integrity. Say this:

"I've heard very good things about The Next Best Company Ever, but all I can tell you are the benefits of my product, idea or service, and the excellent results I've gotten for my customers."

Or...

"I think it's bad business practice to speak negatively about another company. I'd rather speak about the positive results I can get for you with my product, idea or service."

Speaking negatively puts you in a defensive posture and makes you look like you have something to hide. You CAN prop yourself up without putting someone else down. Prospects actually have a lot of respect for salespeople who take the high road and treat others (even competitors) with decency and respect. Who you are with anyone is who you are with everyone. Remember that. Conduct yourself with integrity and people will like you and trust you, and likely, buy from you.

12. BECOMING THE BEST...AND STAYING THERE

If you're reading this book, I'm assuming you have a burning desire to become a sales Outperformer. If you didn't, you'd probably be reading celebrity gossip magazines and hoping people call you with their credit card in hand, ready to place an order (that never happens, by the way). Instead, you're out mastering your craft and proactively making it happen. Kudos to you.

Daily self-discipline and motivation are necessary components to high performance and success. Climbing the mountain is tough...and it's even tougher staying there. You HAVE TO be able to get yourself to do the things you *should* do, even when you don't want to do them. When it's inconvenient and you're unmotivated, you still have to keep climbing. And once you get there, you have to prevent yourself from slipping back down.

You can set two types of goals – performance goals and outcome goals. In short, performance goals are measuring you against your previous standards of performance. Outcome goals measure you against what others are doing. Both can be beneficial (and motivational) if you used the right way.

Outperforming Sales Strategy

Use *both* types of goals to drive your sales results.

Performance Goals:

Performance goals are beneficial because they remove the social pressure and any concern of how you stack up relative to others. This is usually the best strategy because if you spend too much time focusing on what others are doing, you lose sight of what YOU need to be doing.

When setting performance goals, obviously look for a continuous improvement in numbers, but also understand that there are peaks and valleys to every sales situation. You're better off looking at your performance goals based on overall *trends*, like quarterly results. As long as your numbers are constantly improving, you know you're going in the right direction.

It also pays to look at other performance goals that aren't related to numbers. Start tracking how many calls you've made, meetings you've had, webinars you've hosted, and people with whom you've followed up. Most people would call these *process goals*, but they are measures that you have 100% control over and that you can directly wrap your hands around. They are the precursors that drive your sales results.

Outcome Goals:

Most people who are drawn to sales are competitive (many have backgrounds as athletes). They have a desire to win and beat their opponent. So, no matter how much I talk about performance goals, there will always be a time and a place for outcome goals in sales. It's the nature of the industry.

The biggest thing that's wrong with outcome goals is that you only have an indirect control over the result, at best. Think about a sales contest amongst the team. You can have your best sales month EVER but if someone else sells more, you still lose. *That* is the problem with outcome goals and why I'm a bigger fan of performance goals (you obviously would have achieved a performance goal in the previous example).

When using outcome goals, pick someone similar to you (or, preferably, just above you) and have a sales contest. If you're brand new, don't pick the top salesperson. It's too daunting. It would be like the JV team playing against Varsity. You want the person to push you out of your comfort zone but not demoralize you because you look at where they are and think you'll never get there. Studies have shown that using goals that are challenging, yet still realistically attainable, is the best way to fuel self-discipline and motivation. This, in turn, will drive your sales results.

13. CONFIDENCE IS KING

You will never, ever, *ever*, **ever**, EVER find a successful salesperson that is not confident. It's a MUST for selling well.

When you're confident, others believe in you. They know you can lead them. They willingly buy from you. And many salespeople start out confidently but they get beat up so much that they quickly lose it. They start playing not to lose instead of playing to win. They get defensive.

To bolster your confidence, you have to visualize success and have great short-term memory loss. Visualizing success is no different than a professional athlete visualizing a perfect performance. Having it happen in reality starts by first having it happen in your mind. And short-term memory loss comes from quickly moving on when a prospect doesn't buy. I've taught all the people I've managed in sales that, when the prospect says "*No,*" you say "*Next.*" It doesn't pay to dwell on it. There's more to do.

If you struggle to say "*Next*" after someone says "*No,*" you may also not be talking to enough people. Fill your pipeline! Many salespeople get too caught up in a single sale being life or death...but no sale is life or death if you have numerous other options that are just like it. Then if one goes bad, big deal. There's more where that came from.

Outperforming Sales Strategy

Even if you're not 100% confident in yourself (or your product, idea or service) – *fake it till you make it*. APPEAR as confident as possible. Stand up tall, head up, chest out, shoulder blades back and speak with conviction. This type of posture will immediately put your physiology in a better state. How you feel at any given moment can be attributed to your posture.

If you're struggling to visualize success, think back to the last time you were victorious. It doesn't matter how small the win was – ANY win counts. Recall that time as vividly as possible – what did you do? How did you act? What did it feel like? Thinking back to these past victories will put you in the right mindset and emotional state for success.

Lastly, surround yourself with the right people and condition your mind for success. Get rid of the Debbie Downers, naysayers and energy vampires. Never let someone rain on your parade because they have no parade of their own. Spend your time with confident, positive people who will pull you up. And when you're alone, immerse your mind in personal growth and development that will foster an outperforming mindset. NEVER underestimate the power of conditioning your mind for success.

14. BUILD AN OUTPERFORMING SALES BRAIN

Sales Outperformers are able to think quickly on their feet. It doesn't matter how prepared you are or how often you've role-played a sales situation, prospects can (and will) hit you with questions and objections that you never saw coming. It's often in these crucial times that sales are won or lost. You need to be on your game.

Building an Outperforming brain starts by embracing neuroplasticity, which effectively means that you can condition and shape your brain through training. For better or for worse, how "smart" you are and your ability to think quickly on your feet is directly influenced by your daily patterns and routines.

Your goal in sales is to be "on" and to be present during every moment in the sales process. Especially during long meetings or presentations in stuffy office buildings, it's easy to start daydreaming and to let your mind wander. If this happens at the exact time that the prospect asks you a key question, you're in BIG trouble.

Outperforming Sales Strategy

Your goal is to build an Outperforming sales brain that will come through when you need it the most. Just like a car's durability is tested in the most inclement weather, you need your brain to respond in equally difficult circumstances.

Here are four basic tips to build your Outperforming sales brain:

1 – Exercise in the morning

Yes, we've all heard that we need to exercise to improve our body, but exercise is just as beneficial for the brain. There's no substitute for the endorphins that are triggered during exercise and the positive effect these have on our mood and mental focus. Personally, I will exercise *every morning* that I have an important sales call or meeting because I know I HAVE TO if I want to be at my best.

The type of exercise isn't as important as getting your heart rate elevated to the point you're breathing heavily (roughly 75%+ of your maximum), and hopefully, perspiring. The duration can be as short as 15-20 minutes, and if at all possible, take the exercise outdoors. The double whammy of exercise + oxygen from the fresh air is a huge advantage.

2 – Move

The simple act of movement triggers blood flow to the brain. If you're on a sales call, walk around while you're doing it (if you need to be at your computer, just stand up and walk when you can). If you're seated a meeting, exaggerate your hand gestures and sit with your feet flat on the floor (not crossed). If you're waiting in the lobby for the decision maker to meet you, stand up and move. Little things like this MATTER. Movement keeps your neurons firing because when the body turns off (like it does when you're sitting), the brain turns off.

3 – Hydrate

Drink a lot of water. For optimal hydration, I recommend that you have half of your bodyweight in ounces of water each day. So, if you weigh 200 pounds, you'd have 100 ounces of water each day. Only water and/or flavored water counts. No sodas, energy drinks or coffee allowed in this total.

The reason this is important is that blood has to be pumped to your brain via the Central Nervous System and if you're dehydrated from four cups of coffee and no water, it's going to make a difference in your mental alertness and cognitive functioning.

If you're nowhere near the optimal hydration amount right now, build up to it. Start carrying a water bottle with you at all times. Will you go to the bathroom more? Yes. But it's well worth it for knowing you're at your best.

4 – Nourish your brain

Your brain accounts for about 2% of your total bodyweight but it uses 20-30% of the calories you ingest each day. First, your brain cannot function optimally without fuel. You have to give it *something*. Without fuel, your brain is running on vapor and you're not going to be as sharp. Second, if your brain really uses 20-30% of the calories you ingest each day, do you think it's going to function better on cookies and donuts or fresh fruit and fibrous vegetables? You know the answer. Fresh fruit is actually one of the best things you can have before a sales call or meeting because most fruits are not only packed with vitamins (especially B-vitamins, which are good for the brain), they are also packed with water and help with hydration. Similar to exercise, good nutrition is as important for your brain as it is your body.

15. MAKING MONEY AND SELF-SABOTAGING

This will probably be the most introspective part of the book, but are you aware that many people actually don't want to make a lot of money?

Huh? What???

Bear with me here. The easiest way to explain it is with the movie *Titanic*. Think about how the wealthy people in first class are portrayed – they're arrogant, uncaring, unsympathetic and not interesting. They have nothing to talk about and their entire existence seems to revolve around sipping brandy and "congratulating each other on being masters of the universe."

Consider what this does to your psychology. Do you WANT to be wealthy after seeing that movie? And *Titanic* is just one example. There are countless others that have similar themes. Depending how you grew up, you may even have stereotypes of how rich people think and act. This could be from things you saw, read, watched or heard. It may even have come down from what your parents told you.

This amounts to a lot of people self-sabotaging themselves from making money. They have a governor on what they think they're worth and will unconsciously make decisions to keep themselves from whatever they would consider "rich."

If you think I'm full of it, that's fine. But what I'm telling you is the truth and I guarantee if you're not one, you *know* someone who has these beliefs about money. They're usually the ones who say, *"Money isn't everything,"* or *"I don't care about money."* These people usually make enough money to get by, but they're also the ones who usually don't have the disposable income to do the things they genuinely *want* to do. They self-sabotage themselves before they can get to that income level.

Outperforming Sales Strategy

Ask yourself the following question:

"Am I making the kind of money I want to make?"

If the answer is YES, please move on to the next tip.

If the answer is NO, why not? Remember—no excuses, blaming, rationalizing or justifying. If you are not making the money you want (and deserve) to make, WHY. IS. IT. NOT. HAPPENING?

Think about your perception of money and people who are wealthy. Is it positive or negative? Do you see wealthy people as giving and generous, or greedy and insensitive? Your perception is critical.

Now, think about some of the decisions you've made regarding money. If you're in sales and your income level has plateaued for a number of years, chances are you're engaging in some form of self-sabotage. Whatever income level you're at is your governor and you don't want to go above it.

If you're willing to admit that you have some issues with money, start correcting this immediately. Some of my favorite people who have changed the way I view money are T. Harv Eker, Tony Robbins, Brian Tracy and Jim Rohn. Check out any of their books or audio programs and you'll be well on your way to unlocking your true earning potential.

Want access to one of my exclusive sales presentations?

SALES PSYCHOLOGY

I normally don't make my presentations available to the public
but as the proud owner of this book, it's yours.
Complimentary.

This exact presentation was given to a global CRM company on
how to master the psychology of sales.

I hope it serves you.

For Instant Access go to:

OutperformTheNorm.com/books

SECTION 2

PRODUCTIVITY

"You are a collection of your daily decisions,
not your statements."

Ross is at the breaking point.

He's the father of four young kids and has been working 70+ hour weeks for longer than he can remember. The dedication has paid off: he's recently been promoted to the Vice President of Sales for a global medical device company.

As we sit down in his office for our first performance coaching session, the face staring back at me from behind the desk is strained. Like a boxer that has taken too many punches, you can tell the grind has taken a toll.

I ask, "What's your biggest fear in leading this sales division?"

"Getting everything done! I already barely sleep at night and now I have even MORE to do. There are only so many hours in the day..."

I can feel the edginess and overwhelm in his voice. I calmly respond, "Ross, I get it. I've been there. Take a minute before answering this question, but what are the 3-5 things that you have to be *excellent* at to be successful in this position?"

Ross doesn't take a minute.

He immediately blurts out, "I need to be excellent at *sales*! That's my job: to grow sales." His look seems to wonder why I would ask him something so obvious.

"I understand. Growing sales is the end goal. That's the result you want. But how are you going to most efficiently and effectively allocate your time to deliver this result?"

This time, Ross *does* take a minute. His blank stare shows he's searching for the answer to a question he's probably never been asked.

I cut the uncomfortable silence by saying, "The biggest myth in sales, and high achievement, is that Outperformers get more 'things' done everyday. In many cases, they get less done. You will never have more than 24 hours in a day so it's not about completing a longer 'to do' list—it's about prioritizing the RIGHT things. The things that MATTER."

Ross smiles and nods his head in approval. For the first time since we've sat down, he believes there's a light at the end of the tunnel.

If you're reading this right now, you can feel Ross's pain. We've ALL been there: consumed by the number of tasks we need to do and wishing there were more hours in the day to do them.

PRODUCTIVITY identifies what to do, and how to do it, to successfully grow an Outperforming sales business.

16. YOUR FUNDAMENTAL SALES SKILLS

One of the things I preach to all my clients (whether it's an athlete, entrepreneur or business leader) is to be fundamentally sound. There are basic fundamentals to everything in life. Think of a basketball player – the fundamental skills required to play basketball well are dribbling, passing, shooting, rebounding and defense. Your role on the team is going to dictate which of these fundamentals holds more importance but they're ALL required at some level.

Being strong in the fundamentals means you have no weaknesses. When you have weaknesses, you get exposed (usually at the most inopportune times). A basketball player who can't shoot free throws will be a liability at the end of the game. Someone who can't play defense is going to get scored on repeatedly. A player who can't pass is going to miss the open teammate if they ever get double-teamed. You get the picture.

Outperforming Sales Strategy

The basic fundamentals to sales are:

- ✓ **Mindset:** How confident you are, how well you respond to adversity, your overall attitude (positive or negative) and the level at which you *expect* to succeed.

- ✓ **Prospecting**: Your outbound activity, what I refer to as "hunting." Your dedication to contacting new prospects to continually be filling your pipeline.

✓ **Presenting:** How convincing you are and how well you communicate the benefits and overall value of your product, idea or service.

✓ **Following Up:** Your day-to-day activity, what I refer to as "farming." Your dedication to contacting current customers and cold, warm, or hot leads in the pipeline.

✓ **Strategic Planning:** Your ability to analyze your sales segment and develop a strategic business plan to grow your revenue and profitability.

✓ **Technical Knowledge**: How well you comprehend and understand the details and features of your product, idea or service.

To be a sales Outperformer, you HAVE TO know your strengths and weaknesses. We all have things that naturally come easier to us and areas with which we struggle. My biggest weakness in sales was following up. I was great at prospecting and presenting but I was poor at following up with current customers and people who were interested but had not yet purchased. And I got exposed from time to time, usually when an angry customer would get fed up and call my boss directly to say they hadn't heard from me. It was not pretty.

Take an inventory of where you are currently and note the areas where you can improve. Always rely on your fundamental strengths but do whatever is possible to minimize your weaknesses.

17. OWN THE DAY

The hardest part of anything in life is just getting started, but once you're into positive forward motion, momentum takes over and it's easier to sustain it from there.

The specific concept I refer to a lot in my trainings is the "Vital 4%," or the first hour after you wake up (1 hour = 4% of your day). Own the Vital 4% and you will own the day. Don't do it and the day will own you.

Outperforming Sales Strategy

I've asked everyone from dairy farmers to sales directions what the most important things are that we can do in our first hour to set the tone for an Outperforming day. These are ALWAYS the top four responses:

1.   Have an Attitude of Gratitude

More studies are coming out every day showing that the top performers on the planet almost always have the highest amounts of gratitude. They see the good and are driven to contribute with what they have, rather than seeing the bad and being bitter about what they lack.

The best way to do this is by keeping a gratitude journal. Write down three specific things you're grateful for each day, and I promise you, it will shape your entire day thereafter.

2.   Move your body

Exercise is the most powerful performance enhancer for our personal and professional lives. NOTHING else replicates the physical, mental and emotional benefits that we get from exercise.

Beyond the boost in performance, the other benefit to exercising in the Vital 4% is that it's very difficult for life to get in the way when it's one of the first things you do every day. But put it off until after work and all sorts of personal or professional demands can pop up to derail your good intentions.

Oh, and in case you're wondering what the best form of exercise is; it's the one you enjoy the most ☺ Without this, it's going to be very difficult to be consistent.

3.   Fuel your body

Most of us don't link what we put into our body with how it impacts the way we think, feel and perform. Dehydration, low blood sugar (from not eating) and excessive caffeine (too much coffee) can all negatively impact performance. These are only three examples.

Choose a healthy breakfast. Like exercise, I've also realized that almost everyone knows that a banana is healthier than bacon...but that doesn't always mean we'll choose the fruit. My favorite breakfast is a simple meal replacement shake. I can make it in less than one minute and drink it on the way to a morning meeting. It's simple, nutritious and helps me perform better.

4. Plan your day

Brian Tracy once said, "Every minute spent planning saves ten minutes in execution." He's right. Before you get thrown into the storm of your sales day, take 5-10 minutes to ask yourself:

What are the most important things that I need to accomplish today to make it an Outperforming day?

Asking yourself that simple question will help you to focus on the larger goals, projects and tasks, instead of the "busy work" that doesn't necessarily drive our bottom-line sales results.

Be efficient and effective. Don't just work harder; work smarter.

Please note, these are the top four things that I've heard from the thousands of people I've worked with and spoken to. But research has never identified the one "must do" morning routine. It's not as much about *what* you do as it is that you do *something*...and that the *something* serves you in performing your best. The Norm never think about their routines and the impact it has on their results. I'm hoping you will.

18. ONLY TALK TO DECISION MAKERS

The purpose of selling is to make a sale. The only way to make a sale is if someone buys. The only way someone can buy is if they have the AUTHORITY to make the purchase. The person who has the authority to make the purchase is the decision maker.

Only talk to decision makers.

It astounds me the number of salespeople who waste time talking to non-decision makers. What good does that do you? It doesn't matter if the husband has to go home to speak with the wife or if the VP has to speak with the president, spending time with the wrong people gets you nowhere.

If you've been talking to a non-decision maker, your call or meeting usually ends like this:

"Let me speak with Mr. (or Ms.) Decision Maker and we'll get back to you."

Three basic problems here:

1. You should have been speaking with Mr. or Ms. Decision Maker in the first place.

2. You're giving control to someone else (Mr. or Ms. Non-Decision Maker with whom you were just speaking) and letting him/her try to make the sale for you.

3. You probably won't hear back from them, and if you do, the answer is usually not positive.

Typically, the best you can hope for in this scenario is that Mr. or Ms. Decision Maker is intrigued enough to meet with you. Then you have a *chance* at making the sale. But rarely (if ever) will you have someone come back to you saying that they're ready to ink a deal if you've never spoken to the person responsible for the inking.

Outperforming Sales Strategy

Know whom you're talking to. Yes, you can talk to people who aren't decision makers. Often, these people are the "gate keepers" to the decision maker and it pays to get on their good side. But you should be spending the *majority* of your time with people who can BUY.

If you don't know whether you're speaking with the decision maker, here's the key question to ask:

"Is there anybody else you need to consult before making this decision?"

If they say NO, congratulations. You're speaking with the decision maker. If they say YES, you need to do whatever is humanly possible to get in front of this person. Don't let someone else sell your product, idea or service! It doesn't matter how much they like you and how much they believe in you - they will *never* be able to sell it as well as you can.

If the person names someone else, get the person's contact information. If they won't give it to you, ask for a 3-way call or a follow up meeting. If they are reluctant to set this up, let it go and don't force it. But later, go on the company website. You're likely not going to be able to get the decision maker's direct line, but you will be able to get the line of their assistant or secretary. Explain that you just met with Mr. or Ms. Non-Decision Maker and they're considering using your product, idea or service. Say it's extremely important that you speak with the decision maker because there's time sensitive information that needs to be passed along (reference the *Fear of Loss* tip later in this book). Usually, this will be enough for the assistant or secretary to pass you through to Mr. or Ms. Decision Maker.

A secondary option is to send a follow up email to the decision maker. When you're on the company website, scan it for email addresses. Again, the decision maker's email probably won't be listed, but it's pretty easy to figure out. Look at the emails that ARE listed. For example, if middle manager Bob White has an email address of **bobwhite@bestcompanyever.com**, then all you have to do is use the same prefix before the "@" sign and you will get through to the decision maker. Child's play, but you'd be surprised how few people make this connection.

Please keep in mind, all of this can be avoided if your meetings are with Mr. or Ms. Decision Maker initially :)

19. WE ARE WHAT WE REPEATEDLY DO

Aristotle once said, "We are what we repeatedly do. Excellence, then, is not an act, but a habit."

That's selling in a nutshell. It's much more of a marathon than a sprint. Just like you don't get fit for a marathon by running one day, you won't become a sales Outperformer by blowing it up one day either (or even one month, for that matter). It requires the daily training, done CONSISTENTLY, with focus, which gets you to the finish line.

We are creatures of habit and our routines make us or break us. It's the little things we do, stacked up over time, that lead to excellence. We don't notice it in a day and probably won't notice it in a week, either. We'll barely notice it in a month but we'll sure as hell notice it in a year.

Almost all of us have had the unfortunate experience of gaining 10 unwanted pounds at some point in our lives. Maybe it happened over the holidays or maybe it happened when you were going through a tough emotional time. The WHY doesn't matter as much as the HOW. People gain weight because they have a daily caloric surplus (they are taking in more calories than they are burning). But you don't gain 10 pounds in a day. In fact, if you're off by just 100-250 calories, you'll gain 10 pounds in roughly 6-8 months! 100-250 calories is NOTHING. It's a trivial amount. It's cream in your coffee, a glass of wine at night, additional salad dressing for lunch, an extra tablespoon of peanut butter on a bagel, a donut in the morning, a dessert in the evening, etc. This is why you don't even notice it's happening. But stack it up over time and it has a massive effect on your waistline.

The margin of error is so small...in life and in sales.

Outperforming Sales Strategy

What are you committed to doing *consistently* to grow your sales business?

Pick 3-5 things that you will do *every day* to drive your sales results. Make these primarily proactive, outbound activities and DO NOT make them overwhelming. Remember, these are little things that, compounded over time, are going to drive your business. It does you no good to set unrealistic expectations of what you can commit to *every day* and fall short.

Think about sending a couple of emails, or making an extra call. Devoting time to practicing your sales pitch, or studying the competition. Exercising for 15-20 minutes, or carrying a water bottle with you. Planning your daily goals, or analyzing your sales numbers.

Get the point?

A good rule of thumb to know you're doing this right – your 3-5 behaviors should seem almost meaningless, like they're inconsequential (remember, you probably won't notice the results in a day...or a week). But committing to these little things, *consistently*, will have a significant LONG-TERM impact on your sales business.

20. MANUFACTURING URGENCY

Lots of people teach productivity tips like keeping a clean desk and having a "zero inbox" by Friday afternoon, but there is one game-changing strategy that almost no one talks about: Manufacturing Urgency.

Think about the last time you had a seemingly impossible deadline to complete something, whether it was cleaning your house, completing a paper in college or crafting a presentation for a client. Whatever needed to be done, you probably got it done, right? And you got it done because the deadline created an *external* form of urgency.

But, deadlines aside, what if you could wake every day by manufacturing an *internal* form of urgency to fuel your productivity?

Outperforming Sales Strategy

Creating internal urgency requires you to do three things:

1. Clarify the consequences of inaction

We are biologically hard-wired to respond more to feelings of pain and loss than we are to feelings of pleasure and gain. If you don't take action on whatever you know needs to get done (but you may not be doing it), what will that cost you? What pain will you experience because of it?

The more vivid you can make this, the better. Will you get fired? Passed over for a promotion? Lose the business of your top customer? Not be able to take a vacation with your family?

2. Select the causes of complacency

What is the root cause of you not taking more urgent action? More times than not, these are the people with whom you're surrounding yourself. It's very rare that someone doesn't work hard when everyone else around them is doing the opposite. Changing the environment usually changes the level of complacency.

3. Celebrate your small wins

It's hard to have urgency towards something that feels exceptionally far away. This is becoming even more apparent in our society of instant gratification.

The answer is to reward yourself for "moving the ball down the field." Every day, whatever you can do to show that you've made *tangible* progress towards something—no matter how small—is only going to give you more belief in what you're doing, and thus, help you to take more future action.

21. MARATHON SALES TRAINING

My background is as an endurance athlete. I've done five Ironman triathlons and 29 marathons or ultramarathons (at the time this book was written). I don't say this to brag, just that there are striking similarities between sales and endurance training.

Because of my background, I've had a lot of people approach me about training them to get to the finish line of an endurance sport, ranging from 5K's, to ultramarathons, to Ironmans. Usually, these are people who have been in the sport a few years and want to get to the finish line faster.

Getting to the finish line is simple, but I always tell them, "To do something you've never done, you better bring something you've never brought."

Outperforming Sales Strategy

To bring something you've never brought, you need to do two things:

- ✓ Remove any distractions that will get in your way

- ✓ Know which "workouts" are going to bring the best results, fastest

My questions for you as a sales Outperformer are, "What's your finish line and how quickly do you want to get there?"

A small percentage of people have come to me and said they don't care about their overall time, they just want to get to the finish line. So, I put them on a conservative, half-in training program that will get them to the finish line. Everyone gets there EVENTUALLY.

If you don't care about how quickly you get to YOUR finish line (whatever "that" is), then you can have the same approach. But the faster you want to get to your destination, the more you're going to have to remove the distractions in your life that are holding you back from being a sales Outperformer. Maybe it's less TV or happy hours with friends. You're also going to have to focus on the sales activities that bring the best results, fastest, which are the number of calls you're making, presentations you're giving, and meetings you're having.

Remove distractions and focus on maximally efficient "workouts," and you will do something you've never done.

22. THE SWEPT STRATEGY

In the previous point I discussed removing distractions and the best way I know how to do it is to utilize the SWEPT Strategy. SWEPT is an acronym that stands for:

- ✓ **S**ocial Media
- ✓ **W**eb Browsing
- ✓ **E**mail
- ✓ **P**hone Calls
- ✓ **T**ext Messaging

Before I go into the individual components, the SWEPT Strategy was born out of a term called "context switching." This term was originally studied with coders for computer software (a job where it's advantageous to be completely "dialed in") and researchers looked at the amount of time that it took coders to refocus on what they were doing after they had been distracted. The results showed that not only could coders not focus on two things at once but it also took a significant amount of time for them to "switch" back to their original "context" of computer coding. The study has been replicated in other industries, most recently at the University of California-Irvine where it showed the average office worker is distracted every 11 minutes and it takes them 22 minutes to regain concentration.

In other words, we're great single-taskers, not multi-taskers.

Outperforming Sales Strategy

Each of the five components of the SWEPT Strategy could be a book within themselves but peak productivity comes from utilizing these tools to drive, not distract, your sales business. Here are quick ways to use these tools more effectively:

✓ Social Media

The average person spends 2-3 hours on social media each day. To maximize your time, you have to understand the entire purpose of social media is to keep you on their platform *as long as possible*. By keeping you on their site, they can advertise to you and that's how social media sites make money. The deck is stacked against you from the start.

Ask yourself the question when you open up social media, what is the SPECIFIC reason I'm doing this? If it's to send LinkedIn "In Mail," then that's an effective strategy. If it's to read random posts and articles by people, it's not. This reason applies to every platform out there and if you don't have a specific reason, you'll inevitably waste time and be less productive.

✓ Web Browsing

Through the use of "cookies" and retargeting, web browsing can function similarly to social media in regards to advertising distractions. Again, before you start hopping from website-to-website, ask yourself the specific reason you're browsing the web in the first place.

✓ Email

The average person receives over 100 emails per day. Above and beyond the distraction of marketing newsletters from email lists, the biggest time drain from email is notifications. Think about it— if you have a notification that pops up every time you receive a new email, what does this say about how you prioritize emails?

Answer: they're ALL a priority, which means that NONE of them are a priority. Effective email comes from only checking email at specific times throughout the day (yes, this IS possible) and consciously segmenting the emails that are both important and urgent.

✓ Phone Calls

Unless you're in customer service, not all calls are important calls. You need to take your boss's call, your significant other's call, your customers' call and your kids' call, but other than that, phone calls are probably not a top priority.

Again, remember the principle of context switching. If you are sitting down to work on a presentation with 100% singular focus and the phone rings, what happens to that focus? It's lost and it takes time to get it back. Consider silencing your phone during these periods of focused time and setting emergency ringers for the people who are a priority.

✓ Text Messaging

The average text message is responded to in less than one minute. It's a fantastic, fast method of communication with people but it can also be incredibly distracting. The same example can be used as above, and if every text message brings a notification, it's ruining your ability to single task and be maximally productive.

NOTE—I understand SWEPT sounds like a "pie in the sky" strategy. As long as we're doing business with other humans and technology is a part of our lives, this is never going to be a perfect science. But I'm challenging you to audit your time. If you can only level up your focus and productivity *by a fraction*, you will never feel like you have more time and less stress. It's a slight edge principle and I've seen it work wonders for my clients, regardless of title, job description and industry.

23. THERMOMETERS AND THERMOSTATS

I've heard of the distinction between thermometers and thermostats used to characterize leadership styles but it also applies to sales. Thermometers are reactive and respond to what's happening to it. Thermostats, on the other hand, proactively set the temperature in the room.

Proactive, outbound sales activity is the lifeblood of any business. In this way, Outperformers are thermostats. They don't wait for what's happening. They don't wait for the phone to ring or randomly respond to what emails hit their inbox.

Outperforming Sales Strategy

If there's one lesson I've had to learn the hard way in sales, it's this:

**If you're overly concerned with losing a sale,
you haven't done enough to fill your pipeline.**

If you're doing the proper amount of outbound activity, one sale should never matter. There's more where that came from. Unless you're in "inside sales" where your job is more supportive and geared towards growing base business, you MUST ALWAYS be doing outbound activity. Like brushing your teeth, it has to be a part of your daily routine.

My advice for you may seem counter-intuitive, but don't be seduced by what you hear in society about "massive action solving all problems." It may—in the short term—but it's usually unsustainable. Remember:

**What you do every day is more important
than what you do once in a while.**

For example, when I'm focused on growing my speaking business, I will proactively contact 5 people each day about speaking. When I tell people this, they usually look at me like I'm crazy and think that I must be doing something else. 5 people seems like nothing. There has to be more, right?

There's not. But, like brushing your teeth, *I don't miss a day.* EVER. It always gets done, regardless of what I have going on. And I know that if I contact 25 people per week, I will probably hear back from 5 people and it will result in one paid speaking engagement. Based on my revenue targets, that's all I'm after.

I'd encourage you to approach productivity the same way. I don't want to know how many prospecting calls or emails you can send on your PERFECT day; I want to know how many you're committed to sending EVERY day. That's what matters in growing a sustainable sales business.

24. WORK YOUR BUTT OFF

If you want to become a sales Outperformer, you've got to work your ass off. There's no other way. You'll probably need to show up earlier and stay later. You'll need to make the extra call and do whatever it takes to get the meeting.

I know at the beginning of this Productivity section I said that it's not about putting in more hours, but all Outperformers DO have strong work ethic. They continue on when everyone else has given up. It's a prerequisite and, if you're reading this book, my guess it you have it already.

Outperforming Sales Strategy

Ask yourself the simple question:

**"Am I working as hard as I need to work
to see the results I want to see?"**

Even though you will have to occasionally show up earlier and stay later, that's normally not the starting point. Just working more hours won't cut it and my goal is to not have you slave your life away to the sales profession (I actually *want* you to have a life outside of sales). Instead of working longer, the starting point to working your ass off has more to do with increasing your level of FOCUS.

That means when you're working – GET TO WORK! Stop sending personal emails, checking social media, texting your friends, surfing the web, wasting time or doing anything else insignificant to your sales bottom line. Challenge yourself to do this every single day. Set timers and discipline yourself to be as productive as possible in a set period of time. You will be AMAZED at the amount you can accomplish by increasing your level of focus.

25. TWO MOST IMPORTANT DAYS OF THE WEEK

Start fast and finish strong. THAT should be your motto every week you're in sales. If you keep this mentality every week, you're going to be massively successful and more targeted in your actions. It's simply a matter of shifting your focus...and keeping it there on exactly what you want to accomplish.

Outperforming Sales Strategy

Your two most important days of the week are:

✓ Money Making Monday

✓ Follow Up Friday

This means when you wake up on Monday morning, your sole focus is on doing outbound, revenue-generating activities. Take care of the people who may have gotten back to you over the weekend. Reconnect with warm or hot leads that you have in the pipeline. Contact your current customers who should be ready to reorder. Whatever you're doing should be about MAKING MONEY.

You don't have to spend your entire day doing these things, but I always felt like making money on Monday set the tone for the entire week. It got me started fast. It's also a great time to set as many meetings, calls and presentations for the week as possible.

On Friday, your focus shifts to everything that needs to be followed up upon or closed out. Similar to Monday, making a sale on Friday caps off a great week and shoots you into the weekend on a positive note. I mostly like *Follow Up Friday* because we can all be guilty of running around throughout the course of the week and letting things slip through the cracks. Focusing on following up puts us in a mindset of making sure no one drops off the radar. Everyone is moved along in the sales cycle.

Put together, *Money Making Monday* and *Follow Up Friday* are the two most important days of the week for the sales Outperformer. Instead of waking up on Monday and wondering what you're going to do for the week, shifting to a specific focus on these days will yield better results immediately.

26. CONTACTS VS. CONVERSIONS

There are two ways to look at your numbers in sales. First and foremost is the number of new prospects you're contacting and meeting with on a daily basis. When you're new in sales you can expect to have a lot of contacts and less conversions. This is NORMAL and you should not let it stop you. The Norm salesperson thinks that they "just need to know a little bit more," or "do a little more research," before they get started. Nothing replaces getting in the trenches and getting out there. I'm not saying to call prospects and take meetings when you know nothing about your product, idea or service, but I am saying to have the courage to *get started*. There will always be more to learn.

Eventually, as you have more contacts, calls and meetings, your *skills* start to improve. This brings increased *conversions*. In the beginning, you may meet with 5 and get 1. This eventually becomes 2...and 3...and 4. But never 5 – you're not going to sell everyone. It just doesn't work that way.

Outperforming Sales Strategy

Put your self out there! Don't feel like you need to know it all and be comfortable getting uncomfortable. Magic happens outside your comfort zone. In other words...*dare to suck*!

The great thing about sales is that what you lack in conversions, you can make up for in contacts. That's why sales is a level playing field. Even if your initial sales skills aren't very good, you can still be wildly successful simply by contacting more people. This will always outweigh the person who tries to improve their skills and conversions *before* putting themselves out there and contacting prospects.

The mentality that it takes to be successful in sales is to focus more on the process than the outcome. The Norm salesperson is afraid to put themselves out there because they're overly fixated on the result. If the sale isn't made, they get too deflated and link their lack of sales skills as a personal deficiency. If they'd embrace the struggle and the process on the way to mastery, it would free them of not making every sale. They'd know that their skills are continually improving and this is the necessary Price of Admission to be a sales Outperformer.

27. GETTING REFERRALS

Want to know why most salespeople never get referrals?

They never ask for them!

Yes, it really is that simple. Sure, you do have to make sure the customer or prospect is taken care of, but very few referrals are going to be handed to you, no matter the level of quality service you provide. Ask and you shall receive.

Referrals work because it's built in trust and credibility. For the most part, unless you show up and forget how to talk, your chances are *substantially better* of closing a sale where someone else has referred you than if you don't. The person is more at ease and feels better doing business with you because of the third party credibility.

Contrary to what many people think, you don't necessarily have to offer an incentive for referrals. It's not nearly as motivating as people like to think. For some people it will be a motivator (think of the health club that gives a free month's dues if you refer someone), but for the most part, referrals are earned by being likeable, confident and trustworthy. If you have to incentivize someone for giving a referral, the second you take the incentive away, the referrals go away. This isn't the ideal type of customer you want for building a long-term business.

Also, don't think that you can only ask for referrals from customers. You may have just had a meeting where the prospect didn't buy but had a genuine reason for not doing so. Still ASK THEM for a referral. You'd be surprised at how often they drop you a name. As long as you conducted yourself with integrity, there's nothing wrong with still asking the question.

Outperforming Sales Strategy

There is a certain method of asking for the referral that proves best. Here's how you ask for it:

"I know you're someone that people trust, do you know anyone else who could benefit from this product, service or idea?"

(Then stop talking. Let them answer.)

Asking in this way is great because it gives the prospect/customer a compliment (everyone likes that) and it asks a direct question that will elicit a response.

If they say yes, here's what you say:

"Great! Do you mind if I mention your name when contacting this person?"

99.9% of the time if they gave you a name, they're going to have no problem with you dropping their name in a phone call or email.

NOTE – depending on your relationship with the person, you *could* ask them for a favorable introduction to the referral. But be careful! This is a slippery slope. Everyone is damn busy and this could be overstepping your bounds. Remember – you want to make peoples' lives easier...not add more work to their plate. Usually, just mentioning their name in an email or phone call will build sufficient trust.

If they say no, here's what you say:

"Great! If someone comes to mind, I'd appreciate your help and support. I'll also keep in mind anybody who I think could add value to your business."

This response helps in two ways: first, deep down, people want to help and support other people (yes, it's true). The second part preys on the "Rule of Reciprocity," where if you do a favor for someone, they feel a responsibility to do a favor for you. This strategy may not lead to an immediate referral...but it will certainly improve your chances down the road.

28. DO YOUR HOMEWORK

Being able to differentiate your product, idea or service requires that you know what else is available in the marketplace. You should have comprehensive competitive analyses done on all other vendors. You need to know where you're strong (and leverage it) and know where you're weak (and manage it).

In other words, DO YOUR HOMEWORK!

Doing your homework is a critical component to preparation because it minimizes the chance you'll be caught off guard...during a presentation, call, or otherwise. You'll be ready for anything that comes at you, and most of it is strictly a matter of *positioning*. The better positioned you are, the more successful you'll be. But you cannot position your product, idea or service most effectively without knowing what else is out there.

Outperforming Sales Strategy

Create a SWOT analysis on your product, idea or service. If you're unfamiliar with what a SWOT is, here's the breakdown:

S = Strengths

What are the benefits you offer? Where are you clearly superior? What advantages do you have? What do you do better than anyone else?

W = Weaknesses

What could you improve? What do others do better than you? What factors would cause you to lose a sale? What markets (or areas) should you avoid?

O = Opportunities

What interesting trends are you aware of? What changes are happening in the marketplace that you could capitalize on? Are there untapped or emerging markets for your product, idea or service?

T = Threats

What obstacles do you face? What are your competitors doing? How could changes in technology affect your results? Are there any other standards or regulations (government or otherwise) that could influence your sales?

If you've carefully answered these questions, you've done your homework. Also, please note that Strengths and Weaknesses are mostly based on internal factors that are within your control, whereas Opportunities and Threats are external factors driven by market conditions, standards and regulations, and changes in technology.

29. YOUR BEST CUSTOMERS

Who are your best customers?

You might be thinking, "those that have disposable income, those that fit into my target market, those from certain geographical areas, etc."

You're wrong. It's your CURRENT CUSTOMERS.

The hardest thing in sales is getting a new customer to buy. Once they've purchased, it's much easier to keep them loyal and get them to reorder than it is to find another new customer.

Outperforming Sales Strategy

Key concept for every salesperson to understand is LVC, or *Lifetime Value of a Customer*.

When you acquire a new customer, treat them like gold. Almost everyone works with some type of "consumable" product, idea or service. If you're selling toothpaste, people will pay less and consume at a much higher rate than if you're selling computers, but eventually, it's going to come time for a customer to reorder. And they're going to have a choice: stay with you, or find someone better. What they choose is dependent on how you treat them.

What most salespeople don't understand is that customers WANT to stay with you. Everyone on this planet is too damn busy (or, at least they *think* they are) and the last thing they want to do is to go searching for another vendor. So, please don't call or email with this:

"Hi, I'm just checking in to see how everything is going."

To keep customers happy, you obviously have to follow up. My best method of following up is to include VALUE every time you follow up with them. If you *"just check in to see how everything is going,"* there's no value included and nine times out of ten, they won't get back to you. They're too damn busy to tell you how everything is going.

Instead, call or email with something like this:

"Hi, I'm checking in to see how everything is going but I also wanted to include a recent case study of a customer who is using our product, idea or service very well. They're in a very similar position to you and I think you'll find some strategies to really help your business."

How is THAT for providing value and customer service? Not only will they get back to you – they'll be appreciative of you caring enough to make sure they get outstanding results with their purchase. These are the things that sales Outperformers do...and it leads to brand loyalty, ongoing reorders and a high LVC.

30. GET MORE MEETINGS

Most salespeople struggle to get meetings. I hear it all the time, *"The Decision Maker won't get back to me,"* or *"The Decision Maker doesn't want to meet with me."* Why do you think this is happening?

Simple – they don't think a meeting is necessary...or valuable. And this is 100% your fault, based on the way you've positioned your product, service or idea.

You need to understand the mentality of the customer. They HATE to have their time wasted. They don't want "information." They don't want to "learn more." They don't need to be "educated."

What they want is for you to make things *easier*, so they can make more money *faster* with equal or less effort, in a way that is consistent with their company mission and brand, and that will allow them to have some semblance of an outside life as well.

Can you do that?

Outperforming Sales Strategy

How much value are you conveying for the meeting? Why should they meet with you? What are they going to get out of it?

Again, we're not talking about information, learning or education. What are the *tangible benefits* they will receive? Examples (and tell me which one sounds better):

"I'm going to talk to you about how I increased XYZ customer's revenue."

Or...

"I'm going to show you the 5 specific strategies that will increase your company's revenue by 200% in the next year."

Remember—TANGIBLE BENEFITS and increased value. Leverage these and you'll get more meetings.

SECTION 3

PERSUASION

"The art of effective communication is perhaps
the greatest skill you can possess."

"Why aren't more people buying?"

I've been tossing and turning in bed all night and can't get the thought out of my head. I reluctantly grab my phone from the nearby nightstand. It's 2:31 a.m.

I was less than six months into my entrepreneurial journey and earlier that day (or technically, yesterday) I did a 4-hour workshop for a small group of executives. Although the feedback was positive, not a single one of them took me up on my closing offer for a "free performance consultation."

It stings, and at a time when most of the civilized world is sleeping, I'm determined to find the answer. I lift myself from my bed and start walking towards my office. My dog half-opens her eyes inquisitively but chooses not to join me.

My initial thoughts are defensive: it wasn't the right audience. They needed to hear more. It was the wrong offer.

That isn't the truth.

C-suite executives are my perfect audience.

They listened to me for four hours—how much more could they need to hear?

The offer was right. I've never met an executive that doesn't want to perform better.

The problem is ME. I'm not persuasive. My communication is subpar. I love to sell but I haven't mastered getting people to buy.

It's eerily calm in the middle of the night as I sit down to my computer. But before I can even access my training materials it becomes obvious that this goes far beyond my presentation and handouts. It's the way I interact: what I say and how I say it. It's my tonality and body language. My website. My business card. My brochures. My handshake!

All of them are factors in the game of persuasion and influence. I remember the great line, "If all you have is a hammer, everything looks like a nail." My hammer is command and authority. It works quite well...if the prospect is a nail.

I need more tools in my toolbox.

PERSUASION pinpoints the *real* reasons why we buy (and why we don't) and how to best communicate with ALL prospects to maximize your sales.

31. THE FIRST IMPRESSION

You never get a second chance to make a good first impression. Many times people will say, *"don't judge a book by its cover,"* but whether you label it as a judgment or an impression, you form an *opinion* of someone the first time you meet them. It happens in the first 10-15 seconds.

Making a good first impression has to do with three things: how you look, how you dress and how you communicate. Each one is equally important and can (and will) be assessed within 10-15 seconds. It's important that you get them right.

Outperforming Sales Strategy

Here are the must haves for how you look, how you dress and how you communicate:

HOW YOU LOOK

1 – Be Fit

Exercise regularly (at least 5-6 days a week) and include strength training. You don't have to be a fitness physique model, but you do have to be of a healthy bodyweight. Whether they admit it or not, customers are going to wonder whether you can take care of them if you struggle to take care of yourself.

2 – Take care of your skin

Wear sunblock, take a fish oil and multi-vitamin supplement, drink plenty of water and consider juicing fruits and vegetables (you can either go to a juice bar or buy your own juicer and do it yourself). You nourish your body from the inside out and people are more attracted to those with good, glowing skin. Do these things and you'll notice a difference immediately.

3 – Brush and floss your teeth, shave and get a good stylist

In other words, have good personal hygiene. Get your teeth cleaned at least twice a year (or as many as four). Don't be lazy and shave every second or third day. Be clean cut. And men, along with having a good hair cut, make sure they take care of any neck hair, ear hair and nose hair. Seriously – these things matter.

HOW YOU DRESS

1 – If at all possible, buy custom clothes

Custom clothes always fit better than clothes off the rack that are tailored and there are many designers available nowadays who can do pants, shirts and suits affordably. It's worth it to look sharp in something that fits your body type.

2 – Buy nice shoes

Not only is life miserable in uncomfortable shoes, there's no substitute for stunning footwear. You can have everything else right, but without a solid pair of shoes, it's like having a high performance automobile with junk wheels and cheap hubcaps. It diminishes the entire product.

3 – If you're going to wear stripes, make sure they're vertical.

It just looks better. Trust me.

HOW YOU COMMUNICATE

1 – Make eye contact

No eye contact makes you seem uninterested and unconfident. Excessive eye contact makes you seem dominating (and possibly psycho?). Look the person in the eye to make a connection, then take periodic breaks before you return.

2 – Speak up and speak confidently

The first few words out of your mouth should be, *"Hi, I'm Sally Salesperson. It's a pleasure to meet you!"* Now is NOT the time to speak softly. Speaking with authority lets the prospect know that you are comfortable in your own skin and you mean business.

3 – Smile!

You'd be surprised how few salespeople remember to do this. Smiling puts the prospect at ease and even if it's a serious meeting, there's no reason it has to be preceded with a serious introduction. You are happy to have the meeting, aren't you?

Remember – people buy YOU before they buy your product, idea or service. And since you never get a second shot at it, all of these things packaged together are necessary to make an *amazing* first impression.

32. YOUR ELEVATOR SPEECH

Every person who has spent any amount of time in sales has heard of the elevator speech. You're stuck in the elevator with someone and you've got 30 seconds to explain your product, idea or service. How would you do it?

First of all, you don't explain it. There's not enough time. The best thing you can possibly do is to create a connection between what you HAVE and what they WANT.

The problem is, the prospect often doesn't know what they want. No one is going to get into an elevator saying, "Gee, I hope this stranger standing next to me is selling copy machines because that's exactly what I WANT right now."

Yeah, right. Keep dreaming.

Your elevator speech is only meant to serve one purpose: to create INTRIGUE. You want the person to be intrigued enough to give you their business card and when you follow up with them, they'll remember you and agree to meet with you.

Outperforming Sales Strategy

Because you have limited time in your elevator speech, be sure to use any of the following buzzwords:

- ✓ Faster

- ✓ Easier

- ✓ Profits

- ✓ Revenue

- ✓ Cash Flow

- ✓ Impact

- ✓ Growth

- ✓ Purpose

- ✓ Reach

- ✓ Efficient

- ✓ Streamlined

- ✓ Systems

You can customize which of these words will apply to your product, idea or service. From this list, your elevator speech has three basic parts:

**I teach/train/help/show/provide (1) _____
to achieve/accomplish/develop/do/implement (2) _____,
so that (3) _____.**

A sample elevator speech might look something like this:

"I train sales professionals to develop more efficient day-to-day procedures and systems so that they increase their impact and generate more revenue, faster and easier."

Lastly, ALWAYS end with a question or call to action, such as:

"I'd love the opportunity to tell you more about it. Would you have a free 30 minutes for a call or meeting next week?"

Write and rehearse your elevator speech until it becomes natural and second nature. Do this, with a strong call to action, and you'll be able to book a meeting from, literally, anywhere (grocery store, networking event, elevator, etc.).

33. WHAT ARE YOU REALLY SELLING?

Knowing what you're selling is a critical component to sales. It makes sense, right? You're probably thinking, *"Duh, Scott, I'm selling my product, idea or service."* But you're NOT. You have to go deeper than that.

What you're selling is what's underneath the hood. It can be summarized in the simple, "SO THAT," statement. You heard about this in the previous Tip, but it warrants more discussion because this statement is the one that hits the prospect's emotional hot button.

Apple is always one of the easiest examples. Apple doesn't sell computers, phones and tablets. They sell these things SO THAT people can think differently, have beautiful, easy-to-use technology, and go against the status quo. People *identify* with these things and it's about what Apple products DO for them. That's the reason they LOVE Apple and are so loyal to the company. You can't do this with traditional, logical messaging.

Outperforming Sales Strategy

Determine what it is you're *really* selling.

If you're selling a service that will save someone time, what will this time do for the prospect? "You'll have more time SO THAT you're not married to your business, you can have more time with family, you can spend more time on important, revenue-generating activity, etc."

If you're selling a product that's superior to anything else on the market, what will this product do for the prospect? "You'll have a superior product SO THAT you'll gain a competitive advantage, you'll be on the cutting edge, increase your distribution and, obviously, increase revenues."

Of course, you can even look at increasing revenues with a SO THAT statement. "You'll increase revenues SO THAT you'll please your shareholders, you'll become a debt-free company, you can boost employee morale by giving additional bonus incentives, you'll have more cash flow to fund future strategic initiatives, you'll sleep better at night, etc."

Again, you'll notice that almost all of these things mentioned after the SO THAT statements trigger emotional responses because it goes deeper than features vs. benefits. It gets into the WHY people are doing business in the first place. If you haven't already done so, think about your SO THAT statements surrounding your product, idea or service and leverage them accordingly. You'll see the difference immediately.

34. PEOPLE HATE INFORMATION

One of the worst things you can ever say to someone if you're trying to get a meeting is "I want to give you some information on blah blah blah." Information is everywhere. Have you ever heard of Google? You can have millions of pages of information at your fingertips within seconds.

I can't tell you the number of newbie (and veteran) salespeople I've heard talk about "information" like it's the holy grail of selling. If information was the primary driver of sales results, we could send out white papers and scientifically validated studies to all of our prospects and the rest would be history.

Please understand – it has NOTHING to do with the amount of information, and too much information is actually *bad*.

Again, you have to realize the mentality of the prospect. Before you even open your mouth, they're already too damn busy for *whatever* you have to offer. So, if you start hammering them with massive amounts of "information," they're only going to perceive it as adding more to their already full plate. They'll say no every time.

Outperforming Sales Strategy

People don't want information – people want a professional recommendation with a focused plan of action.

Example – I purchased a new computer from Best Buy a couple weeks ago. I entered the store, walked straight over to the Geek Squad guy and told him what I wanted:

"New computer. Reasonable price point. Don't care about memory because all of my data will be stored in the cloud. Lightweight. No other bells and whistles necessary."

From there, he walked me over to the computers and told me what to buy based on what I *wanted*. He could've walked me in circles around the computer section, shown me five different computers and given me information on each, but instead he made a professional recommendation and I trusted him. He knows a lot more about computers than I do (the same way you know a lot more about your product, idea or service than the prospect does).

Now, you likely don't have prospects walking up to you, telling you *exactly* what they want. I understand that. But a large chunk of this book centers around listening and asking key questions, and if you do this properly, people will tell you what they want. Then, it is up to you to make your professional recommendation with a focused plan of action by positioning your product, idea or service as a SOLUTION. Whatever you do, don't feel the need to give them more information. Everyone has an "information threshold" and The Norm salesperson frequently exceeds it.

35. COMMAND YOUR PRICE POINT

Many unconfident salespeople fear selling products, ideas or services at higher price points. Their perception is that all buying decisions are based on price and this is the only driving factor for the prospect. It's part of the reason that The Norm salesperson will struggle to sell more expensive "packages." They either lack confidence in their product, idea or service, or themselves, or all of the above.

The solution: **Command Your Price Point.**

First, you have to understand and appreciate how the customer views your product, idea or service. What do you want to be compared to? A higher price point isn't about robbing someone of more money than something is worth – it's about an emphasizing the *quality* of your product, idea or service. The higher the quality, the more expensive something will be.

Think about Mercedes vs. KIA. Or Whole Foods vs. Cub Foods. Or Apple vs. Microsoft. Or Target vs. Wal-Mart. There is certainly a difference in the quality of the product being sold but there's an even bigger difference in your *perception* of the quality. One brand is perceived as common and cheap, the other is perceived as prestigious and expensive. This perception drives the buying behaviors of customers based on how they see themselves and how they want to be seen by *others*.

Outperforming Sales Strategy

Know whom your ideal customer is and how you want to be seen in the marketplace. Customers with a higher socioeconomic status aren't looking for discounts and will happily pay for things that have value. On the other hand, customers with lower socioeconomic status are usually driven by price and are looking for deals and discounts. Neither one is bad but The Norm salesperson thinks the world is their oyster and thinks *everyone* is their target market. If you market to everyone you market to NO ONE.

I first noticed this when I managed personal trainers. In most affluent areas, the average rate for personal training is probably $70 per session. I couldn't believe the struggle that new personal trainers had selling at this rate. They didn't believe in themselves and they weren't able to command their price point. They thought their prices should be lower, not realizing that the type of people who typically hire personal trainers are those who *want quality* and are willing to pay for it.

I now see many of these trainers running $5-$10 boot camps, which means you had better pack the class or you're going to struggle to be profitable. I also see these same offers being made on daily deal sites, like Living Social and GroupOn. I can set up the same boot camp down the street, charge $25, only need half the people (and thus, half the headache), be seen as a higher quality brand and be more profitable. You choose how you want it.

There is nothing wrong with offering inexpensive products, ideas and services...if that is truly your target market. Only you know your ideal customer. But if your goal is to attract higher end customers, you must adjust accordingly and command your price point.

36. STOP DISCOUNTING!

When I walked into my last sales job, we were the kings of discounting. We had different "tiers" of pricing that were *supposed to* be based on the volume of products purchased, but it had become commonplace over the years for the sales force to automatically discount products, regardless of whether the customer had the necessary volume to qualify for the discount. It was a mess.

So, for my entire first year, I went along with what everyone else had done...and was doing. I liberally discounted our products for anyone and everyone. I was just happy to make the sale! In the down economy of 2008, I finished at 98% of my annual quota, which was still best amongst the Regional Account Managers.

I'll never forget sitting down with my boss for my annual review in January and him saying that if I just would have *minimized* my discounts (still discounting, but not discounting *so much*), I would have finished at 105% of my sales quota, which would have meant A LOT of extra money in my pocket. UGH!

I had never stopped to look at it this way. I thought I had to discount or I wouldn't get the sale, which is part of the reason that I kept doing it (and the reason that most salespeople discount in general). But I learned a valuable lesson that day and everything changed in subsequent years when I no longer relied on automatic discounting to make sales.

Outperforming Sales Strategy

If you are discounting, stop it! Or stop doing it SO MUCH!

Don't get stuck in the mindset that you have to discount or the prospect isn't going to buy. If you're doing your job and adding value, you won't need to discount to make the sale. You'll be able to command every penny of the full price for your product, idea or service.

Also, even if you lose a few sales (which will undoubtedly happen because you'll have people who will only buy if they're "getting a deal"), minimizing your discounts means you'll have greater profit margins so you need to make less total sales to make the same (or more) income. This should be refreshing and empowering!

If you are someone who is in a spot like I was, take a step back and ask yourself whether you genuinely NEED to be discounting as much as you are. Is this a market reality or your own self-created fantasy? Give it a sustained period of time (3-6 months, minimum) where you actively try to minimize discounting and see what it does to your sales results. I'm confident you'll be pleasantly surprised.

37. THE POWER OF SOCIAL PROOF

We all have a certain level of skepticism when it comes to trying something new. It's natural and ingrained in our psychology. The way to combat this is by demonstrating social proof.

If you'd like to do a quick experiment, for the next 24 hours count the number of times you see a billboard, radio or television advertisement, review, testimonial or satisfied customer story about a product, program or service. They are EVERYWHERE and there's a reason why: when we see others get results with something, we say to ourselves, *"If it worked for them, it will work for me too."* It chips away at our skepticism. It's powerful and that's why all companies do it.

Outperforming Sales Strategy

Two considerations for using social proof in sales:

1. Make it prominent

It doesn't matter your business or your industry, if someone has gotten results using what you offer, highlight it. There's no disadvantage to doing it. You can use any of the before mentioned strategies on your website, social media platforms or print marketing. Using stories of social proof in your sales presentations is also extremely effective.

2.   Make it relevant

Have you ever watched an infomercial for an exercise product? Without a doubt, they'll have the person leading the workout and 2-3 other people of VARYING fitness levels doing the workout as well. They use this same strategy in the testimonials regarding the effectiveness of the program.

The reason why they do this is relevance. If I'm watching the workout but my fitness level isn't nearly as good as anyone doing it, I will think it doesn't apply to me. I'll skeptically think, *"It worked for them but it WON'T work for me."* The more relatable you can make your social proof, the more persuasive it will be in your sales business.

38. DON'T BE DESPERATE

I don't know a lot about women (yes, yes, it's true!) but I do know that the desperate guy doesn't get the girl. Women are attracted to a man with confidence, who knows what he wants and is sure of himself. Not outright arrogance...just quiet *confidence.*

Sales is EXACTLY the same way.

The Norm salesperson that settles for any prospect that gives him/her the time of day will probably never make the sale. The prospect can spot a desperate salesperson from a mile away. How do you expect a prospect to have confidence in your product, idea or service, when you don't have confidence in yourself?

Outperforming Sales Strategy

Believe it or not, one of the best mentalities to have in sales is that you have to *agree* to do business together. They don't have to agree to do business with you. You also have to agree to do business with them. You enter into the agreement TOGETHER.

What this does is takes the pressure off you as a salesperson. You're not trying to convince them. They also have to convince you. It's all about the vibe you put out. Even if you desperately want to make the sale, it's better to make the impression that you know what you want and the type of people with whom you want to do business.

You may be saying, *"But, Scott, I want to do business with everyone. I've got a sales quota to hit!"* I get it. I've been there. But you actually DON'T want to do business with everyone. Two clear-cut examples - if your product, idea or service is unnecessary or wrong for someone, don't sell it to them. The short-term commission might be nice but when they realize you sold them something they don't need, it'll come back to bite you. The second example is if the prospect is a pain in the ass. NO amount of commission is worth this, because if the person is a pain in the ass *before* you've made the sale, it's going to be even worse *after* you've made the sale. You should enjoy the people with whom you do business. There are plenty of them out there.

A key phrase to use is, *"The specific reason I'd like to do business with you is because of..."* This shows that there is a specific reason you're speaking with them. You've done your homework. You know what you want. Prospects will respond positively to this phrase. Men, can you imagine walking up to a woman and saying, *"The specific reason I'd like to date you is because of...?"* Ha! Let me know how that works out for you :)

39. WHAT MATTERS MOST (THE BLT)

People buy from people they believe, like and trust. Really, this is all it comes down to. If you have these three things, people will often buy from you, even if your product, idea or service is inferior to something else on the market.

The reason this happens is because buying decisions are driven by emotions. As hard as we may fight to remain logical, that's simply not how human beings are wired. The single best thing you can do to enhance your sales results is to become more likeable, confident and trustworthy.

So, it begs the question, which one(s) are you lacking? If someone isn't buying from you (assuming that your offerings aren't *vastly* inferior to everything else out there), one of these things needs to be improved upon.

Outperforming Sales Strategy

Determine what needs to be strengthened and do the following:

To be more likeable:

Build more rapport. You HAVE TO find a common ground and a way to relate better to people. Think of all the people you don't like in your life – chances are, you don't relate well to them. You don't have a common ground. You can't understand where they're coming from.

Finding a common ground with a prospect can be any of the following (these are only a few examples):

✓ Sports teams

✓ Hobbies

✓ Area where you grew up

✓ Similar vacations (look at the pictures in their office)

✓ Family and number of kids (also look at the pictures in their office)

✓ Church or community activities

✓ Reading interests (look at the books on their shelves)

If you're not confident (i.e., they don't believe in you):

Start with your handshake (see *The Wet Noodle Handshake* tip). Then, focus on your preparation and homework. Preparation brings familiarity and familiarity brings confidence. I would also recommend recording yourself on audio and video so you can critique your own pitch and performance. Again, this will be a brutal experience at first, but it will greatly enhance your confidence.

To be more trustworthy:

Why are you doing what you're doing? And, more specifically, WHOM are you doing it for? Are you just trying to make a sale or are you genuinely recommending what you feel is in the best interest of the customer?

People can see if you're full of sh*t from a mile away. They will be able to tell if you're putting your own personal interests in front of theirs. Always remember to have a service mindset, provide exceptional value and make it about the customer FIRST. Sales are simply a byproduct of doing what's right.

40. BE BOLD

Remember that person you met a while back who walked and talked and acted just like everyone else?

Neither do I.

To be a sales Outperformer, you must be bold. You must be memorable. You must be DIFFERENT from everyone else out there.

Bold does not mean arrogant. You can be bold and different and still be humble and well intentioned. And CONFIDENT. Confidence is arrogance under control. You become arrogant when you feel as though you know it all and there is nothing new to learn.

To be bold, realize that it's a one shot deal. Sorry to put the pressure on you but you don't get a second chance. You can't go in purring like a kitten and then start roaring like a lion. It doesn't work. It's incongruent. Be bold from the first minute.

Outperforming Sales Strategy

The most important area to be bold is in casting vision and presenting the benefits for the prospect. You've got to OWN IT. This doesn't mean lying to them and saying you're going to double their business overnight, or this is the greatest idea in the history of mankind and the only one that will work for them. It does mean to speak in a way that sets you apart and makes them believe in you.

Again, consider the kitten and the lion. Here's the kitten:

"This product will greatly increase your company revenues."

"This service is going to enhance your employee morale."

Here's the lion:

"If you employ the step by step process with the product I'm recommending, you can expect to see a 50% increase in gross profits by this time next year."

"Your employees are going to have less sick days, higher engagement and greater productivity with this service. And you know what that will translate to for you? A coveted company culture and an improved bottom line."

Be bold. Be convincing. Be memorable. If you believe in your product, idea or service THAT strongly, others will too.

41. GIVE AND YOU SHALL RECEIVE

Have you ever been at a grocery store that was giving out free samples and you walked up to the table to try it, even though you knew, deep down, that you had no intention of buying what they were offering? When you walked away from the table you probably felt some sense of guilt that you weren't going to buy, right? That you took something and didn't give anything back?

This feeling represents the psychological principle of Reciprocity, which states that when we are given something, we feel obligated to give something back in return. It's part of the reason that companies will do a no-risk "try before you buy" and "even if you don't like it, you can keep part of it as our special gift to you." Companies do this because they know if they give you something up front, you'll have a stronger pull to give them your business in return.

I can even think of times that I walked into a grocery store, couldn't find what I was looking for, but tried a free sample and bought something from the store anyway, for no other reason than I felt badly about taking a free sample and not giving them anything back in return. Now, THAT is reciprocity!

Outperforming Sales Strategy

What can you give, big OR small, to a sales prospect that will increase the likelihood that they'll give you their business? I'll give you three examples:

1. I started leasing a new vehicle recently. When I walked into the dealership, the first thing the—smart—salesperson did was to offer me something to eat or drink before he even asked me what car I was interested in.

2. Whenever I contact businesses or organizations for which I'd like to speak, I ALWAYS give them something up front. It's usually an article or video that is specific to their industry and some of the challenges they may be going through. I give them value.

3. Give a good old-fashioned—sincere—compliment to someone with whom you'd like to do business. Simple as that.

You might look at these things and think they're insignificant but by giving *something*, big OR small, of value in each of the examples, it's more likely that you'll receive something (a sale) in return.

42. A CONFUSED MIND SAYS NO

One of the biggest mistakes rookie salespeople make is thinking more information will translate to more sales. This thought process leads them to hammer the prospect with facts, figures, details and otherwise insignificant junk instead of what actually drives buying decisions.

You've probably heard of the K.I.S.S. principle, or *"Keep it Simple, Stupid."* It's absolutely true...ESPECIALLY in sales. Sales are based on the prospect seeing themselves using your product, idea or service. Simply stated, if they are too confused by what you saying to them, they'll never be able to see the "after picture." They'll be stuck in the before...and they'll say NO.

Outperforming Sales Strategy

Keep things as simple as possible and paint a crystal clear picture of taking the prospect from Point A to Point B. Don't include superfluous information unless it's essential to their success.

One of the best ways to ensure you don't confuse the prospect is through examples and case studies. Walk the prospect through, step-by-step, exactly how you helped someone in their similar situation. They'll be able to insert themselves into the story and will be more engaged. If you're just starting out and you don't have any relevant case studies, create a sample customer lifecycle and the results they can realistically expect from using your product, idea or service.

Next, use visuals – they always help create a simpler, more compelling story. More and more companies are advertising through services like VideoScribe, where you've got a hand drawing pictures on a whiteboard to illustrate a story. There's a reason why they do this and why it's so effective – it keeps people engaged and the visuals help people to be able to see themselves in it.

You don't have to have a VideoScribe done about your product, idea or service (though it may not be a bad idea) but it's a good reminder of the thought process you should have in sales. ALWAYS keep it simple, and when you're done talking to a prospect, are you confident they'd be able to walk you through the Point A to Point B of using your product, idea or service? If not, simplify it even more!

43. LISTEN, DUMMY!

The sweetest sound for every person is the sound of their own voice. Let it be heard! But you'll never be able to hear it if you don't stop talking!

Basic sales training is based on the 80/20 rule, in that you should listen 80% of the time and talk 20%. Of course, it never works out this way (or, at least, I'm yet to see it) but it is a good thing to keep in the forefront of your mind – you should be asking questions instead of launching into an endless soliloquy.

The critical reason it is so important to ask questions and listen is to find out what makes the prospect tick. The more you can learn about them, the better. You can use the information to build rapport and to tailor a better offer based on what you learn about the prospect. There's no downside to letting the prospect talk...other than it requires more time. But it's well worth it when you end up with the sale.

Outperforming Sales Strategy

Ask as many open ended questions as you can. If you don't know what an open-ended question is, it's something that cannot be answered with a yes or a no. In other words, something that makes the prospect "open up" himself or herself and elaborate on what they're thinking.

As good rules of thumb:

✓ Starting with *"Do, Can or Will,"* usually leads to close-ended questions.

✓ Starting with *"How, Why or What,"* usually leads to open-ended questions.

Pay attention to how you're phrasing your questions. Almost all close-ended questions can be tweaked to be open-ended questions.

✓ **Bad:** Do you know what direction you're looking to take your business this year?

✓ **Good:** Why is it important to you to take your business in a different direction this year?

✓ **Bad**: Will you be making a buying decision today?

✓ **Good**: How can I earn your business today?

✓ **Bad**: Can you see yourself using our product, idea or service?

✓ **Good**: What are your thoughts on using our product, idea or service?

The more open-ended questions you can ask, the more the prospect will talk, the more you'll learn about what makes them tick, the more you can tailor your message to their needs, the higher your sales conversions and the greater your level of future success.

How does that sound to you (an open ended question)?

44. THE 3 COMMUNICATION COMPONENTS

In 1967, a study was done at Stanford University on persuasion and communication. Of course, this study is getting a little outdated but it has been replicated many times since. Many people think *what you say* is the most important thing in persuasion and communication (and sales, for that matter), but the study found something totally different.

When a message is communicated, certain things matter more than others. Based on the percentages, here's what REALLY matters when it comes to persuasion:

7%: What you say

38%: Tonality (volume and pitch)

55%: Body language and physicality

What does this mean to your sales results? Simple - WHAT you say matters less than HOW you say it.

If you're looking to persuade and communicate better with prospects, start worrying less about what you say and worry more about how you're saying it. Pay attention to your tone and your volume. Have a proud posture and a body language that exudes confidence, yet openness. These things are both vastly overlooked when it comes to the sales process. Traditional sales trainers want to give you sales scripts and "closing techniques" to deliver sales. And the results these yield are negligible.

Outperforming Sales Strategy

Here are three strategies to deal with each of the components of persuasion and communication:

Tonality:

Everyone with a cell phone made in the last 5 years has a microphone and audio recorder on it. One of the best ways to know how you sound when you're with prospects is to record yourself practicing different aspects of the sales process (recording and reviewing a live conference call is even better). Your tonality should be confident, but not aggressive. It should be inviting. At all costs, try to avoid being monotone by varying the tone and pitch of your voice (not just your volume!). This will keep the prospects more engaged in meetings, calls and presentations.

Body Language:

Have an open, engaging body language. Hands in pockets means you lack confidence. Arms crossed in front of you means you're closed off. Hands on hips means you're confrontational. Simply have your hands at your side or have your hands resting on one another. And use gestures! It makes you seem more alive, passionate and persuasive. Shoot yourself on video if you want to know how you really look when you're with a prospect.

What You Say:

If you are still intent on focusing on the 7%, follow these cues:

- ✓ Tell stories: some people think stories don't have a place in business presentations but they DO. Stories interspersed into a presentation make your product, idea or service relatable to the prospect and create a connection for them.

- ✓ Speak to benefits: Always focus more on the end result of what something will DO, rather than what something HAS. Benefits move people emotionally.

- ✓ Ask open ended, bold questions: Get the prospect talking AS MUCH AS POSSIBLE. How do you see your business growing over the next year? Why is that important to you? What are your strengths? Weaknesses? If you could change one thing about your business, what would it be? Who do you see as your biggest competition?

This is a subtle distinction that most people don't recognize about sales Outperformers. The Norm salesperson focuses on what they say, Outperformers focus on how they say it. Prospects always respond more favorably to the latter.

45. SELLING WITH SCARCITY

Basic buying psychology says that when there is less of something available, we want it more and deem it more valuable.

Think of the last time you booked a flight to go somewhere. Whether it was through Expedia, Orbitz or directly through the airline's website, you probably saw something that said "only 1 seat left available." Because the seats on the airline were scarce, it increased your incentive to buy.

Outperforming Sales Strategy

There are two ways to create scarcity:

1. Limited inventory

This is the type of scarcity with which most people are familiar (and it's the type used in the example above). If you truly have a limited inventory of your product, program or service, highlight this for people. It works in, literally, any industry and is a fantastic way to persuade people. Let people know when it's gone; it's gone.

IMPORTANT—I have seen a rise in "false scarcity" online in the last few years. For example, people telling you to reserve your seat for a webinar because they have limited capacity. Or encouraging you to buy an eBook because there are "only xx number of copies available." C'mon now. That's insulting the customer's intelligence and people are getting tired of it.

Only use limited inventory to persuade if your inventory is truly limited.

2. Uniqueness

If you offer something online or a specific product, program or service that doesn't have limited quantities, the other way to create scarcity is by demonstrating your uniqueness. You may have heard this as your USP, or *Unique Selling Proposition*.

Think of higher-end cars, hotels, restaurants, clothing brands, technology, diamonds, etc. Yes, there may technically be "limited inventory" of these things, but the big draw that pulls people to buy is the uniqueness. They are distinct in their industry, and because of this, we see them as more valuable.

What makes you unique and different from what others are doing? Be as specific as possible and highlight this point.

46. CALLS THAT GET RETURNED

Remember the basic principle: people HATE to have their time wasted. Even the process of listening to a :30 second voicemail will annoy them if they feel like you're wasting their time.

This is the type of voicemail The Norm leaves:

"Hi, this is Scott Welle from The Best Company Ever. I was hoping to talk with you about our new service that could greatly enhance your company's profits. Please give me a call back at 800-867-5309 at your earliest convenience. Again, that's Scott Welle from The Best Company Ever at 800-867-5309. Have a good day."

Blah! You sound like all the rest and you wasted my time. Do better!

First, give some specifics about what you're offering – not the features, the *benefits*. Next, say something that makes it look like you did your homework ("*I noticed in your quarterly newsletter that you're rolling out these new initiatives*"). They'll appreciate you taking the time. Lastly, give specifics when you're speaking about growth, profits, costs, etc.

Outperforming Sales Strategy

There are two types of voicemails you can leave. Sometimes, less is more. If you already have a relationship with the person and you really need a call back, leave the following voicemail:

"Hi, John, this is Scott Welle from The Best Company Ever. Can you please give me a call back at your earliest convenience at 612-990-1756? Thanks. Bye."

It's counter intuitive and most people won't leave this voicemail because they believe they have to give the person more information. But this voicemail actually creates intrigue, and the customer starts wondering why you're calling. I've found this is a better option than leaving a lengthy voicemail with information they're potentially not interested in – you'll NEVER get a call back that way. They're not going to call you back to tell you they're not interested...they just won't call you back. Better to do anything you can to get them on the phone – then you stand a fighting chance.

Obviously, this has to come after you've met the person, built rapport and established some type of relationship. You can't call a complete stranger and ask them to call you back without saying why you're calling and expect that they will return your call. But, in the right situation, this "Less is More" voicemail works better than you'd think.

The next voicemail is a better version of the typical voicemail The Norm leaves:

"Hi, this is Scott Welle from The Best Company Ever. I would like to speak with you about our new service that can grow your company's gross profits by 86% in the next 12 months. I just had a fantastic meeting with XYZ Company and I thought it would benefit you as well. Please give me a call back at 800-867-5309 so we can talk details. Again, that's Scott Welle from The Best Company Ever at 800-867-5309. Have a good day."

A few highlights of what makes this better:

✓ "I would like to speak with you"

Much more direct and compelling than, "I was hoping to speak with you."

✓ "Grow your company's gross profits by 86% in the next 12 months"

Specific, tangible measures of improvement. Sounds much more concrete than, "could greatly enhance your company's profits."

✓ "Just had a fantastic meeting with XYZ Company"

Social proof that other people are doing it. Creates a fear of loss that if they don't hear about it, they may miss out. Even if you haven't had a meeting yet, say you have an upcoming meeting with someone (assuming you actually do). If you don't have any meetings coming up, pick up the phone and get to work!

✓ "Thought it would benefit you as well"

Wow, really? That's so nice of you and I appreciate it. I'm intrigued.

✓ "So we can talk details"

Makes you sound like you're a person with a plan. People WANT that. If they're going to call you back, they should know that you've got something in mind for them that they can follow. People hear, *"at your earliest convenience"* all the time. Trust me – people can (and will) find an extraordinarily high number of things that are more convenient than calling you back.

Overall, use this voicemail if you have no relationship (or a weak relationship) with the customer or prospect and you know you need to give them a little more information than the "Less is More" voicemail.

47. IMPACTFUL FOLLOW UP

One of the most important aspects of sales is follow up. Speaking from personal experience, you can do this right and you can do this WRONG.

Two important points:

1. Be Prompt

When you get done with a call or meeting, prompt follow up is *critical*. Whether you realize it or not, it says something about YOU. It says something about the way you treat your customers (even if they're not your customers yet). If you're not timely with your follow up, they'll believe that this is how you're always going to respond, and even if they're not your customer yet, they'll believe that even when/if they DO become your customer, they'll be treated with the same lack of urgency. Not good.

Your goal should be to make them feel like they're the most important customers you've ever had. Everyone wants to feel valued and it'll pay off better for you in the long run. If it all possible, follow up the same day. At the bare minimum, follow up within 24 hours. If you have a lengthy proposal to draft, at least send them a short, concise "Thank You" for their time and set the expectation of when they can expect the proposal.

2. Be Distinct

Being memorable is what matters. The person who blends into the crowd is not the one who gets chosen. Even if the prospect doesn't do business with you immediately, when the time is right and they are budgeting for a new service (for example), the person who is the most *distinct* will be the one with whom they choose to reconnect and do business.

Outperforming Sales Strategy

Prompt follow up speaks for itself. Get it done and get it done fast. No exceptions. Being distinct can go two separate paths:

OLD SCHOOL: Send a handwritten note

Handwritten notes are quickly becoming a thing of the past. Almost no one sends them anymore. But they make an IMPACT. And the impact they make is to say that you're willing to take the time to write a letter, stamp it and put it in the mail, instead of just draft an email. No one can write as fast as they can type so it says their business is worth you taking additional time to do something you could have done faster, and easier, through email. Still send the normal (prompt) follow up email and let the handwritten note that is delivered a couple days later be the double whammy.

NEW SCHOOL: MailVU video mail

MailVU is one of the best services I've come across for video mail. Let me say this – technology is changing so rapidly that there's a decent chance at the time you read this, there may be something else out there that is bigger and better, but I chose MailVU because it's easy and affordable.

This is how it works – every reasonably new computer has a webcam (it also has an app for phones). So, instead of sending a stale email, you record a short video and send it to the prospect or customer. It plays on all computers and on all phones...and people LOVE IT. Every person I've sent it to has come back and has raved about how "cool" it is. Similar to the handwritten note, it provides a personal touch from you to them, and makes you distinct in the process. Win, win.

48. PERSUASIVE PRESENTING

Learning to give persuasive sales presentations is a skill that can be mastered. Even if you're not standing in the front of a formal conference room with a projector and whiteboard, you are almost certainly presenting your product, program or service in some way. This is "game time" for sales professionals and it pays to know how to maximize this time.

Outperforming Sales Strategy

There have been entire books written about how to do effective sales presentations but these are four of my best tips:

1. Tunnel their attention

Imagine you're selling a new software program for B2B sales. You meet with a potential customer and you can ask them one of the following two questions:

  ✓ What do you like about your current software?

  ✓ What do you dislike about your current software?

Which one do you think it more effective? It's the latter.

Cialdini calls this "attention tunneling," where you get a prospect focused on the things they dislike about a current situation, and thus, they become more open and willing to make a change.

2. Use the 'Rule of 3'

The Rule of 3 is everywhere:

It's as easy as 1, 2, 3...

A, B, C...

Gold, silver, bronze...

When in doubt, give people 3 options (a "good, better, best").

If one option is given, the prospect may feel too confined. It will feel like a "take it or leave it decision" and you don't want them leaving it.

If two options are given, many prospects will often choose the lower option and you're giving up valuable revenue and margins.

If four options are given, it's too many for the brain too handle (see *A Confused Mind Says NO*).

Three options are perfect and you will find that most prospects will choose the middle option. The key is to structure it so you're happy with the sale you're making and the customer feels satisfied.

3. Anchor the Price

Every time you look at a price, online or offline, and see one price written, but then crossed out, and another lower price written next to it, you have seen an example of price anchoring. Companies and salespeople will do this so you feel like you're getting a "deal" by being able to purchase at a lower price. They've anchored in a price that's higher than what you're actually paying.

This may go without saying, but any time you're anchoring a price (and especially when doing the Rule of 3), make sure to state your highest price FIRST. Then, anything the prospect hears after it will feel better by comparison.

4. YOU > I

The word "you" is one of the most persuasive words in the English vocabulary, yet it's drastically underutilized in sales presentations. The Norm is very comfortable using "I" and "we" to describe what their product, program or service will do for a prospect but are not as comfortable using "You," usually because they feel preachy when they say it. But being preachy comes much more from the tonality than from what you're actually saying (see *The 3 Communication Components*).

When you're rehearsing your sales presentations, count the number of times you say "You" vs. "I."

Say, "Are YOU ready for the best sales software in the industry?" instead of "I will present the best sales software in the industry."

Or, "YOU will receive the 50 Best Tips EVER for growing your sales business," instead of "I will give you the 50 Best Tips EVER for growing your sales business."

Changing one small word can yield BIG results.

49. ASKING KEY QUESTIONS

The best salespeople know that what you *ask* is every bit as important as what you *say*. The more you can get a prospect talking, the more dirt you can uncover about what they like, what they hate and, most importantly, what YOU can do about it. That's what Outperforming salespeople do – they use the information the prospect gives them as ammunition to favorably position their product, idea or service. This is why you should ask key questions in almost every sales call or meeting.

Why else is asking key questions so important? Plain and simple, decision makers will lie to you. They don't always mean to do it (sometimes they do) but usually they won't tell you exactly what they're thinking or feeling. People are polite...especially in the Midwest. They'll hide it and say something like, *"Let me think it over,"* or *"I'll get back to you next week."*

Newsflash – they've already thought it over. And they won't get back to you next week. If you don't ask some key questions you're probably going to lose the sale.

Outperforming Sales Strategy

Here are the top five key questions you can ask during a sales call or meeting:

1. What keeps you awake at night?

Ask this question early. Warning – you never know where the answer is going to go. For example, the prospect may respond perfectly by talking about revenue or margins (which gives you a perfect opening to position your product, idea or service as a solution), or they might go off on a tangent about useless employees or a company picnic that went bad. You never know...but either way, you're better off asking the question.

2. What would it take to double your business next year?

This is a key question to ask and you'll be surprised how few people know the answer. Usually best to ask this question early on as well, and especially if they don't know, insert what you have as a solution. This is a winning formula.

3. What would your objections be to not doing business with me?

Traditional sales books may steer away from this question because they think it gets the person focused more on the negatives instead of the positives, but I personally love it. Ask this question towards the end and, usually, the prospect will give you a straight answer. If I feel like they're not, I'll say, *"C'mon, you don't need to bullshit me. Just give it to me straight."* (smile or laugh when you say this) Then, once you have their objections, you can easily combat them or come to a compromise. If you can't come to a compromise, then you weren't meant to do business together in the first place.

4. If you could change one thing about your business, what would it be?

Best to ask this question somewhere in the middle, or after you've built a certain amount of rapport. If you ask it too early, you'll probably get a surface answer that isn't truthful. You want to know something they would *really* change if they could. Similar to question #1, this response could go in a lot of different directions, but you're always better off knowing the answer.

5. Are you happy with your level of business success up to this point?

This is kind of a trick question, and you will find, very few people are happy. It's not a question that it intended to make the prospect feel bad, but it will uncover some of the things they would like to improve and any mistakes they've made in the past. Almost EVERYONE (especially Type-A business owners) would like to be more successful than they are today. Ask this question early and get the prospect talking.

You don't have to ask all five of these questions in every sales call or meeting. In fact, if you do, it might be overkill. Just ask the ones that you feel most comfortable with...but I would recommend asking at least 2 of them. These key questions will uncover the information that you can leverage to make more sales.

50. CLOSING

Most sales books will have at least one chapter dedicated to "closing techniques." Usually, this includes different phrases you can use at the end of a call, meeting or presentation that will lead to the prospect making a purchase.

These techniques are all well intentioned but they're meaningless if what you've said up to that point is subpar. Think back to the girl in high school who you always wanted to date. You can't be awkward and stumbling all over yourself and then expect the perfect closing line is going to land you the date. Sales is similar. Even the best closing technique in the world won't get a prospect to buy if they don't like you, believe in you and trust you (as well as your product, idea or service). What you do leading up to the close is much more important that the close itself. Don't forget that.

Outperforming Sales Strategy

This entire book has been about strategies to enhance your products, ideas and services, so I'm going to assume you're following them and you're set up with a legitimate shot at making the sale. IF you are in this position, knowing how to close DOES help.

This is going to come as a shock to you, but The Norm salesperson usually doesn't make the sale because they don't ASK for the sale. They just end the meeting hoping that the prospect will say they want to buy so they don't have to feel uncomfortable asking for it. It's incredible. The point of sales is to sell and if you never ask the prospect if they want to buy, how do you expect to get the deal? Very few prospects will outwardly say they want to purchase. You have to make the effort to pose the question.

The type of personality I'm talking to usually drives the question I will ask at closing (assuming I haven't had the rare meeting where the prospect *tells me* they're ready to get started now). If you're speaking with a Type-A dominant personality, ask them this:

"So, what do you think?"

Pretty simple question, right? They know you mean *"What do you think about doing business with me,"* but you don't need to say that. And the reason you keep it short and vague is because dominant personalities don't like to be backed into a corner. They're comfortable making quick, decisive decisions if you let them. If they feel like you're not allowing them to do this, you'll lose the sale.

If you're speaking with a more laid back, casual personality, ask them this:

"Would you like to get started today?"

Again, the question is short and sweet. You want to present the casual personality with a question where they have to make a decision. If you're in front of this type of personality and you leave the meeting without a clearly defined plan of action, you can waste months going back and forth before they'll make a decision. Better to just ask them for it and see where you stand.

In the corporate world, most of the people you'll be speaking with are in the Type-A category. They got to where they are because of their ability to make decisions. If you're selling direct-to-consumer, you'll run into a lot more people who are casual and need to be moved to action. This isn't pressuring them – it's just simply asking them to make a decision out of respect for your time and energy.

THE BEST OF THE REST

Want even more Outperforming sales strategies? Here are 10 additional tips to help your psychology, productivity and persuasion:

51. KILL 'EM WITH KINDNESS

Basic sales law dictates that you catch more bees with honey than vinegar. In layman's terms, be nice to people. It'll pay off for you (literally and figuratively).

This probably sounds like the simplest, most obvious sales tip in the book, but many things are simple and obvious – that still doesn't mean we DO them.

Kindness means treating other people the way you would genuinely want to be treated. It means showing up on time, being polite, having manners and being respectful.

Outperforming Sales Strategy

Here's your checklist for *Killing 'em with Kindness*:

Showing up on time:

Leave earlier and always arrive at meetings 10-15 minutes ahead of time. If you are going to be late, call or text the prospect *as soon as possible.* At least, then, the expectation has been set, rather than letting the person sit around twiddling their thumbs waiting for you. But time is precious – if you want other people to respect your time, it starts with respecting theirs.

Be polite:

Say please and thank you. Look the person in the eye when you say these things. Let them know you mean it.

Have manners:

The best way of showing you have manners is by being a better listener. Don't interrupt the person when they're talking! Wait until it's your turn to talk. Along these same lines, LISTEN to what they're saying when they're talking. Many poor listeners pre-determine what they're going to say long before the person has even finished what they're saying. When you do this, you lose the true message and the conversation has less flow.

Be respectful:

This one is simple – always do what's best for the person...not what's best for your paycheck. If you start doing things and operating on what's best for you, any amount of short-term gain is going to be magnified by a long-term loss. Make recommendations and sales based on what they *need*, not what you *want*.

52. THE WET NOODLE HANDSHAKE

You never get a second chance to make a good first impression.

99.9% of sales meetings are going to start with a handshake, regardless of whether you've previously spoken on the phone or corresponded via email. It's the way we introduce ourselves, especially in America. The handshake usually comes before you've even had a chance to say your first sentence. You can't win a sale with your handshake but you sure as hell can lose it.

I don't want to go too voodoo on you, but when you touch someone there's a connection and a transfer of energy between them and you. And, in sales, you're probably not going to have any other point of physical contact with the prospect than from your handshake. It's important to get it right.

A proper handshake requires finding the appropriate amount of pressure with which to shake hands. Your job is to MATCH the pressure from the prospect. It is kind of like dancing – you need to match your partner's rhythm.

A firm handshake displays confidence and command, but it's not necessary to dominate them and death grip their hand. This will rub them the wrong way from the get-go. On the other hand, a limp wet noodle handshake shows a lack of confidence and belief (either in yourself or what you're offering). Prospects will be able to *feel it* before you've even spoken a word. Finding the balance between these two extremes is key.

Outperforming Sales Strategy

An Outperforming handshake actually contains 3 essential components:

1. Match the pressure of the handshake to the pressure exerted by the prospect. Handshakes match peoples' personalities. If you pay careful attention, you can probably guess the pressure of their handshake beforehand, based on how they walk and how they initially talk. Faster walking and louder talking will have a much firmer handshake, and vice versa. Just respond to what they're doing.

2. Usually, you'll be shaking hands at the same time you'll be introducing yourself. Say to the person, *"Hi, my name is [insert name]. It's a pleasure to meet you. Thank you for your time."* An additional add-on to this is to say to what company you represent after you say your name.

3. Look the person in the eye! Don't look at the floor and *please* do not look at their hand. Making eye contact also displays confidence and lets the prospect know that you are comfortable, self-assured and that you mean business. Looking at the floor makes it seem like you're afraid or have something to hide.

Think these things don't matter? Consider:

Much of psychology is based around the Primacy and Recency Effects. These effects state that, when you're meeting with someone, you're going to ALWAYS remember the first things and the last things better than you will what happens in the middle. And considering most meetings begin and end with a handshake, it pays for you to get it right...because it's what they'll remember the most. This was also discussed in the *Your First Impression* tip.

53. RADIO STATION WIFM

If you've never heard of this radio station before, please allow me to fill you in: Radio Station WIFM is the one everyone listens to, and if you want to connect with and understand people better, you need to check it out.

WIFM = What's In It For Me

(Maybe that makes it WIIFM, but you get the picture)

I don't say this as a claim that everyone is selfish. They're not. It's just the way people are wired. Especially in sales where most prospects are hyper sensitive to slimy salespeople with ulterior motives, you need to make a concerted effort to point out what's in it for THEM, or they're never going to hear your message (and you'll never make the sale). This goes beyond pointing out the benefits of your product, idea or service – it's about constantly keeping your focus on what's in it for the prospect.

The other reason remembering Radio Station WIFM is important is that most salespeople are excellent talkers. And talkers love to talk...about *themselves*. You think you're helping or building rapport when you do this, but you're not. You're just boring the prospect while they sit there wondering, *What In It For Me?*

Outperforming Sales Strategy

Take a piece of paper and write down all the reasons the person should do business with you. Really brainstorm on these points! You should be able to come up with at least six rock-solid reasons on what's in it for them. If you're able to come up with more, that's great. Prioritize them in order of what you think would interest the prospect the most. Then, it simply becomes a matter of you emphatically stating these points *early*...and reiterating them *often*.

54. USE HUMOR

Traditional sales and advertising will tell you to stay away from humor. They want you playing conservatively (basically, playing *not to lose*) and want to make sure you don't offend anyone. Their rationale is that you don't need humor to make a sale. It's not required.

That's great. I also don't need spice to eat my food but it tastes a helluva lot better to me than if it's bland.

Many people think humor needs to be directed at someone else or some *thing*, but one of the best ways to use humor is to poke fun at yourself. If you're bald, make fun of it (*"sorry I'm late, I was combing my hair."*). If you're short, joke about being vertically challenged (*"I didn't meet the height requirement to get on the bus this morning."*). This lightens the mood and adds a human element to sales. It's very tough to go wrong when the humor is self-directed. This adds...ding ding ding...LIKEABILITY!

Regardless of how serious and stuffy an atmosphere may seem, no one *wants* it that way. Sure, the prospect may be there to get things done, *fast*, and not have their time wasted, but that doesn't mean they don't want to smile while they're doing it.

Adding humor into a presentation also makes you more memorable. It sparks a different variety of emotions. You always remember a roller coaster more than a train ride.

Outperforming Sales Strategy

Hopefully, I do not even need to say this but be SMART about how you're using your humor. Never use humor about:

- ✓ - Gender

- ✓ - Race

- ✓ - Ethnicity

- ✓ - Sexual Orientation

- ✓ - Political Affiliation

Most people are extremely sensitive about these things and if you stay clear of them, your humor will go over well. Even if you think you know the person well enough to be able to make these types of jokes, DON'T. If it doesn't go over, you can never take it back. Distasteful humor can undo any amount of rapport, belief and likeability, and ruin any sale. Proper humor, on the other hand, lightens the mood, relaxes the atmosphere (and prospect) and helps you make sales.

55. NEGATIVE EXPERIENCES KILL

A short time ago, I had a company call me that specialized in reputation marketing. Reputation marketing is your overall brand presence online and what people are saying about you. It's surely an industry that didn't exist ten years ago.

We did a Google Hangout to chat about it and, even though I didn't end up hiring them, I did see the validity in what they were selling. I can tell you from firsthand experiences that people are buying more and more everyday based on what *other people* are saying. Reviews are powerful and ratings are crucial.

Now more than ever, negative customer experiences KILL your business. Most of my books sell on Amazon and for every one negative review I have, I need 8-10 positive ones to counterbalance it (please remember this when you're reviewing this book!). The rest of the online world operates exactly the same way. If someone is unsure whether they're going to purchase something, the first place they'll turn is not what the company says about the product, idea or service – it's what *other people* are saying. They'll likely Google it to find out, which gives you very little control over what is actually being said.

Outperforming Sales Strategy

People are going to have negative experiences and talk badly about your company. That's inevitable in any industry. You can't please everyone. But your goal is to *minimize* these experiences as much as possible.

Most of the time, this has to do with the follow up and level of customer service after a sale is made. Even if someone doesn't like your product, idea or service, they'll likely still talk nicely about it if you do everything in your power to make sure they have a good experience. The harsh, negative reviews happen when the customer feels like they've been taken advantage of and nobody cares about them. This is why they act out and post negative reviews...because they KNOW somebody will care about that.

This may seem like a time drain and an awful lot of work to make sure customers are happy (especially if you don't have the processes in place to efficiently make this happen), but it's worth it for the long-term growth of your business.

56. A CLOSED MOUTH DOESN'T GET FED

Introverts struggle with sales. Intuitively, that probably makes sense. If you are uncomfortable talking to people, it's difficult to sell. The same way that a closed mouth doesn't get fed, a mime typically doesn't get a lot of sales ☺

People are surprised to know that I score directly in the middle between introvert and extrovert on almost every personality inventory (most think I'd be a heavy extrovert). This means that being outspoken and social in all situations is often not my style. I had to LEARN to communicate this way when I needed to. In sales, it's imperative. If you're anything like me, it's a communication style you must learn as well.

Outperforming Sales Strategy

Join a speaking group, like *Toastmasters*.

There are *Toastmasters* groups all over the world and they're extremely affordable. The groups are dedicated towards helping people become better speakers. People in the group critique your speaking and you have the chance to do the same. Speeches are done on different topics each week and all speeches are allocated a specific amount of time.

If this sounds intimidating, GOOD! It was for me when I did it too! I went to a small group of about six people (none of whom I knew) and put myself out there. It was extremely uncomfortable at first but I knew it would make me better. With each passing week, I learned more about speaking and, more importantly, *communication*.

There's no substitute for getting collective feedback from a diverse group of people. I also appreciated the fact that all speeches were timed. It keeps you concise and keeps you on task. If Mr. Decision Maker tells you he only has 30 minutes to meet, you better not waste 29 minutes blabbing about your product, idea or service. You need to know how long your presentation (or "sales pitch") will last and be able to stick to those guidelines. Then, you can budget in time for answering questions, overcoming objections or, hopefully, inking the sale at the end of the meeting.

Always remember – the things we want to do the *least* are almost always the things we need to do the *most*. Outperforming sales is (and always will be) about your ability to communicate effectively. Investing your time and energy will pay off in big returns.

57. FEAR OF LOSS VS. STRENGTH OF GAIN

Basic psychological studies state that people respond more to a fear of loss than the strength of gain. In other words, people will often move to action faster if they feel they're "missing out." This becomes a powerful positioning tactic for the sales Outperformer.

Every single person reading this has probably seen an infomercial of some kind. All infomercials are structured the same way in terms of benefits, testimonials, warranties, etc., but every infomercial will also end with time sensitive bonuses being revealed at the end, usually with a countdown clock that prompts you to take action. As this clock is counting down, the person pitching the product, idea or service, will tell you that these bonuses are, *only available for a limited time and once they're gone, they're gone!* Buy now or you miss out.

What does this mean?

Outperforming Sales Strategy

This is what a fear of loss vs. strength of gain sounds like:

Fear of loss:

"The top 3 companies in your industry are already implementing my product/idea/service, and I don't want you to get left behind and lose market share."

Strength of gain:

"Using my product/idea/service will keep you competitive with the other top 3 companies in your industry."

It's a simple shift in positioning and using this language sounds counter intuitive. People should respond to the positive and what they hope to gain, right?

Not so much.

People will make decisions, move and buy more based on what they're losing more than what they're gaining. Use this to your advantage when you're speaking with a prospect! In addition to the language you're using, if you don't already have them in place, find creative ways to implement time sensitive offers that you can leverage to create a fear of loss, such as bonuses, add-ons, 2-for-1's, discounts, packages, extended warranties, early bird specials, or anything else that will move a prospect to action to avoid missing out. I'm not a fan of perpetual discounting (see *Stop Discounting!* tip in this book) but using the right type of discount, with the right type of customer, to create a fear of loss is worth it.

58. KNOW WHEN TO STOP

At the time this book is being written, there is a hot show on network television called *Shark Tank*. Basic premise of the show is that it brings in entrepreneurs to pitch their product, idea or service to the "sharks," who are a handful of self-made millionaires (and billionaires). The entrepreneur starts out by asking for a specific dollar amount for a stake in their company (i.e., I'm looking for a $100,000 investment in exchange for 25% ownership in my company). The sharks will listen to the sales pitch and if they like the idea, they will invest in the company. But they almost NEVER invest the initial amount the entrepreneur is asking for – they give their best offer on what they feel the company is worth. It's very much a "take it or leave it" mentality.

Sales professionals can learn a lot from watching this show, not only from a numbers and a company valuation standpoint, but also from a communication perspective. When the sharks make a counter offer or ask a hard question, they say it with confidence and they shut up afterwards. They don't keep talking because they're uncomfortable with the silence. They let the entrepreneur stew in the discomfort and look him/her dead in the eyes because they know, the next person who talks, loses.

Outperforming Sales Strategy

Know when to STOP!

When you ask a difficult question or make an offer, say it with strength and stop talking afterwards! Let there be a moment of uncomfortable silence. This moment is necessary where the prospect collects their thoughts and decides whether or not to move forward.

The Norm salesperson can't live here. I've seen it a thousand times. They think the silence is a bad thing and they need to fill it with more convincing details and idle chatter. This usually has the opposite effect – it makes you appear uncertain of the recommendation or of the question you just asked, and the prospect gets lost in what you're saying.

The foolproof way to know whether you're doing this is to listen to yourself. Replay meetings and conversations in your head. If you started by asking a question, then immediately followed it with a barrage of details, you have not learned the skill of shutting up when it matters most. Here's what it looks like:

The Norm:

"What are your thoughts on moving forward with My Most Awesome Product Ever? Because I really think it would be a great move for your company. It would give you a leg up on the competition and you'd be on the cutting edge. Plus I'm willing to give you volume discounts and an extended warranty package."

Outperformer:

"This would be a great move for your company. It would give you a leg up on the competition and you'd be on the cutting edge. I will give you volume discounts and an extended warranty package. So, what are your thoughts on moving forward with My Most Awesome Product Ever?"

Outperformers stop talking here and NEVER say another word until the prospect does first. It's a simple reversal of information but it means EVERYTHING. Outperforming salespeople are great talkers...but they also know when to shut up. And the time to shut up is after you've asked a critical question.

59. VARY YOUR VOICEMAIL

Does your voicemail sound something like this:

"You've reached the voicemail of Scott Welle with Outperform The Norm. Sorry that I'm unavailable to take your call but if you leave your name, number and a detailed message, I'll be sure to return your call as soon as possible. Thanks and have a great day."

Very professional and very polite. Also very BORING.

Your voicemail is just like your business card – it should be distinct and stand out. Almost all voicemails sound the same. There's nothing unique about them. Believe it or not, your voicemail says something about YOU too...and because you're the one representing your product, idea or service, your voicemail becomes a natural extension of these things as well.

See where I'm coming from?

Your voicemail should show your sense of humor (if you don't have one, that gives you something to work on). If the person leaving the message is still laughing when they start recording, you've done your job. Making them laugh makes them like you. Even if they're not laughing, using your sense of humor will at least make them *remember* you.

Outperforming Sales Strategy

Try these sample voicemail scripts:

"This is Scott Welle with Outperform The Norm, but if you're calling, I'm guessing you knew that already. So, why don't I just stop talking so we can get to the beep and you can leave your extremely important message? Cheers!"

"This is Scott Welle with Outperform The Norm. Recent studies have shown that 40% of people use Caller ID as a tool to screen their calls, but that's just rude. I'm genuinely unavailable. But please leave your name and number and I'll get back to you ASAP."

"This is Scott Welle with Outperform The Norm. I'm out changing the course of our entire human civilization with my product, idea or service. If you'd like to join in, or knock some sense into me, please leave your name and number. Enjoy the day!"

Don't be afraid to be bold and to use your own voice! I guarantee the prospect will remember you after any one of these voicemails. They are samples of things I would say (and have been on my actual voicemail) but if they sound unnatural to you, change it! BE YOU! You want to sound funny and casual. Don't be afraid of sounding unprofessional. Trust me, people hear enough automated, dry or boring voicemails every day that it is actually refreshing to hear something that doesn't sound like everything else.

Other recommendations:

- ✓ DON'T tell people what day it is on your voicemail. Do you think they're living in a cave? They know what day it is!

- ✓ DON'T tell them their call is extremely important to you. They should know that already.

- ✓ DO tell them if you're out of the office. It will set the expectation that you may not get back to them as promptly.

- ✓ DO record a voicemail message. There's nothing worse than calling someone and hearing the automated voicemail recording. First, you wonder if you called the right number (at least I do). Second, we talk to enough damn robots as it is – let people hear your voice! It makes it personal...and makes you human.

60. ELEVATE THE PROFESSION

Lots of people have a negative perception of sales. Chances are, they had a bad experience with a shady salesperson that was trying to pressure or manipulate them and it left a bad taste in their mouth. They've never gotten over it and now they believe every encounter with a salesperson is going to be just like that one.

In reality, we've probably all had a run in with a slimy salesperson at some point in our lives. People who care more about selling than sharing and caring. People who will sell unnecessary things just to boost the price of a sale (and their commission check). People who claim personal, ongoing follow up, but after the sale is made they're nowhere to be found. People who mislead prospects with empty promises about what their products, ideas or services are truly capable of doing.

Yes, we've all been there. It gives the sales profession a bad name.

I believe sales is the best profession on the planet. Commission is the fairest form of compensation for Outperformers. You work, you get paid. You make sales, you get paid. You slack off, you don't get paid. There's less incentive for people on nothing but a fixed salary to give their maximum effort because their income is guaranteed. I always appreciated the fact that I could make as much as I wanted to make in sales. I'm sure you appreciate that too.

Sales is also the most important driver of our economy. If times get tough, companies can make cuts to almost every department *except* sales. Without sales, the company makes no money. They won't even be able to keep the lights on and doors open. Companies need sales...and you're an integral part of making this happen.

Take pride that you work in sales...and DO IT THE RIGHT WAY.

Outperforming Sales Strategy

Be one of the good guys (I'm sure you are already if you're reading this book), have people's best interests at heart and do whatever you can to elevate the profession. Every sales Outperformer who does this helps to correct any negative misperceptions. It IS possible to do what's best for the prospect AND to be phenomenally successful in the process.

Constantly work on your skills. Strive to become a better communicator, develop processes for better implementation and follow up and savor the fact that you're part of the rare breed that can succeed in sales. Outperformers are unique...and you're one of them.

CONCLUSION

I started this book emphasizing that selling contains SKILLS. The best salespeople have worked harder, and smarter, to refine their sales skills. It's a process of constantly tinkering and tweaking, seeing what works and what yields the best results. It's never a "finished product." Sales Outperformers are the ones who are always looking for areas to improve, whether it's a different method of explaining a benefit or a new way of positioning their product – there's always something that can be potentially done better.

I didn't know it at the time, but my best sales training came early on when I first started as a personal trainer. Like most health clubs, each new member was offered two "complimentary personal training sessions," which were geared towards basic goal setting and a general overview of an exercise program using the facilities' equipment. This was an opportunity for me to sell the member my personal training services that would help them get better results, faster and easier.

I learned A LOT about selling...in a short time. First, people don't care how much you know until they know how much you care. 99% of the new members couldn't care less that I had a Master's degree in Kinesiology and multiple certifications. They just wanted to know if I could help them lose weight (or whatever their goal happened to be). It also taught me the skill of casting vision. I had to get the person to see, and believe in, a better version of themselves. For the most part, none of them wanted to know the detailed explanation of *how* the process worked – they only really cared about the finished product, what it would look like, how it would make them feel and how it would benefit their life. I've carried these lessons with me to every sales situation I've been in since.

If you want to be a sales Outperformer, it always comes back to the BLT (*Belief*, *Likeability* and *Trust*). Start by embracing the struggle (and process) on the way to mastery. Even if you're frustrated and feeling beaten down right now, know that it, too, shall pass. There are always people who will climb the ladder and have more "natural talent" for sales, but one of the biggest contributing components to sales results is likeability, which is a *learnable* skill. Most people are blind to the fact that they may not be likeable, so it pays to ask someone where you measure up and things you could potentially improve. Inevitably, it will start with building stronger rapport and simply listening and asking more questions, instead of interjecting your own opinions. Remember – the sweetest sound for everyone is the sound of their own voice.

If you're a likeable person but you're still not getting the results you want, you probably have a belief issue...in yourself. Read more books, listen to more podcasts and watch more videos on personal growth and development until you have conditioned your psychology for confidence and success. DON'T STOP UNTIL YOU'RE THERE. This is the foundational layer and if you're consistently underperforming in sales, this is an area you need to work on (even if you don't *think* it is). The secondary layer on top of this is your preparation and homework. Most of us will lack confidence in doing things we've never done and the more you can mentally, and physically, rehearse a given sales situation, the more you'll feel like you've "been there and done that."

Lastly, be trustworthy. Be who you say you are. Be on time and if you say you're going to deliver something, you better damn well do it. Trust is a fairly simple thing – every time you do what you say you're going to do, you gain trust. Every time you don't, you lose trust. There is no in between. You're either progressing or regressing. Trust is also doing what's right for the customer. Don't sell what's best for you, your paycheck or your quota – always sell what's right for THEM. One negative experience will outweigh 8-10 positive ones but the surefire way to minimize negative experiences is to always do what's right for the customer, be prompt with your follow up and make sure they feel appreciated.

The last piece of advice I'll leave you with is this – be authentic and true to yourself. I've never been a fan of telling people what to say (remember – *what you say* has less impact than *how you say it*) because when people start trying to say things that are unnatural for them because they *think* it's what the prospect wants to hear, it ends up backfiring. The best sales script in the world can't overcome you trying to be someone you're not. You're better off being relaxed, natural and comfortable in your own skin. The tips in this book are flexible enough that you can incorporate them into your own unique style. And, as long as this style is presented with belief, likeability and trust, you'll be putting your best foot forward towards being a sales Outperformer.

To your outstanding sales success,
Scott

ABOUT THE AUTHOR

 **SCOTT WELLE** is a #1 international best selling author, speaker and founder of Outperform The Norm, a global movement that coaches athletes and business leaders to raise their game and perform at the highest level.

While the rest of the competition is playing not to lose, Scott teaches people to play to win. His proprietary "Commit / Attack / Conquer" formula ensures people fall asleep at night knowing they are making the most of their precious days on this planet. For this, Fox 9 in Minneapolis-St Paul has called him a *"Motivational Expert."*

Scott has always loved sports but felt he underperformed early in his career by not mastering the "mental game." After graduating with his Master's degree in Sport Psychology, he made it his life's mission to coach people to higher levels of performance and not let others repeat his mistakes. Throughout this process, he's realized how the same mental principles that allow athletes to be successful will allow business leaders to achieve exceptional results, and this formed the foundation for Outperform The Norm.

Now, Scott's eight best selling books, articles, videos and podcasts inspire hundreds of thousands of people worldwide and students in over 35 countries have taken his online courses. He is an adjunct professor at St. Olaf University and serves on advisory committees of three national level organizations. He regularly coaches top performing executives, sales professionals and entrepreneurs, as well as elite athletes, all with one common goal: to OUTPERFORM.

Scott enjoys pushing his own physical and mental limits, completing five Ironman triathlons, 29 marathons, R2R2R (47 miles back and forth through the Grand Canyon) and a 100-mile ultra marathon run. He is very close with his brother, Jason. Together they "plod" at least one marathon together each year, laughing the whole way.

Please visit him at ScottWelle.com.

ALSO BY SCOTT WELLE

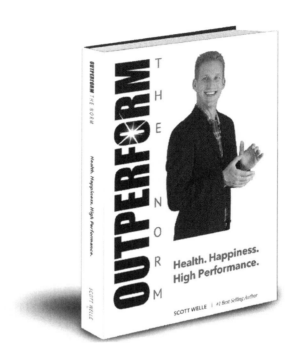

OUTPERFORM THE NORM

Health. Happiness. High Performance.

OutperformTheNorm.com/books

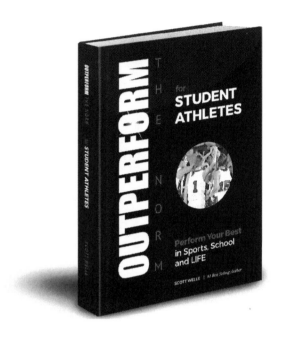

OUTPERFORM THE NORM
for Student Athletes

Perform Your Best in Sports, School and LIFE

OutperformTheNorm.com/books

OUTPERFORM THE NORM
for Network Marketing

Six Steps to Six Figures This Year

OutperformTheNorm.com/books

Made in the USA
Middletown, DE
04 April 2019